Jayson Tatum: The Inspiring Story of One of Basketball's Rising Stars

An Unauthorized Biography

By: Clayton Geoffreys

Table of Contents

Foreword

The end of the Big Three era for the Boston Celtics meant a new core had to be established for the storied franchise. The Celtics found themselves with a collection of valuable draft picks, which enabled them to build that very core. In the 2017 NBA Draft, the Celtics selected Jayson Tatum. Since joining the league, Tatum has quickly established himself as one of the more promising rising stars. Just twenty-three years old at the time of this writing, Tatum has consistently demonstrated his versatility on the court. The story of how he made it to the NBA is even better. Thank you for purchasing *Jayson Tatum: The Inspiring Story of One of Basketball's Rising Stars*. In this unauthorized biography, we will learn Jayson Tatum's incredible life story and impact on the game of basketball. Hope you enjoy and if you do, please do not forget to leave a review!

Also, check out my website at claytongeoffreys.com to join my exclusive list where I let you know about my latest books. To thank you for your purchase, you can go to my site to download a free copy of *33 Life Lessons: Success Principles, Career Advice & Habits of Successful People.* In the book, you'll learn from some of the greatest thought leaders of different industries on what it takes to become successful and how to live a great life.

Cheers,

Clayton Geoffreys

Visit me at www.claytongeoffreys.com

Introduction

The NBA style of basketball has often gone through different evolutions and transformations throughout its history. From its earliest days when big men ruled the paint in a fast-paced style that did not have a three-point line, NBA basketball transformed into a more structured defensive style of play in the '70s. Then, during the '80s and '90s, the game became more physical as teams relied more on a grind-it-out style that involved a lot of one-on-one, man-to-man defense.

During the 2000s, we saw teams relying more on superstars as names such as Kobe Bryant, LeBron James, Dirk Nowitzki, Kevin Garnett, and Dwyane Wade emerged as players you can give the ball to if you want your team to get buckets. This steadily transitioned into a different style of play over the next decade as franchises began to create super teams with three or more All-Stars.

However, though there are still super teams in today's era, the style has become more reliant on overall team play instead of just putting the ball in the hands of the team's three All-Stars. We saw the Golden State Warriors playing that way since they won the NBA title in 2015. Though they had many stars on their team, they relied more on spacing and ball movement to win games. This led to the current pace-and-space era, where teams rely more on increasing the game's tempo while spacing the floor with four or more shooters.

This pace-and-space era led to the introduction of position-less basketball that demands all five players to bring the ball up, make plays for others, and shoot the ball from the perimeter. You are now seeing frontcourt players 6'7" or taller spacing the floor with their three-point shooting or even playing the point from time to time.

On offense, everyone needs to shoot and create plays for others. Meanwhile, everyone should switch out on either quicker players out on the perimeter or big men inside the paint on defense. This led teams to stock their rosters up with players capable of playing multiple positions on both ends of the floor.

In that sense, some of the most sought-after talents in the NBA today are wings capable of playing offense and defense as either backcourt or frontcourt players. We saw the Golden State Warriors winning titles with 6'7" Draymond Green playing center and 6'11" natural small forward Kevin Durant scoring from the outside but defending the paint over at the other end. We also saw Kawhi Leonard getting All-Star selections and winning Defensive Player of the Year as a player that can defend positions 1 to 4 in the NBA.

Used to playing forwards all their lives, tall and long wings such as Giannis Antetokounmpo, Paul George, and Ben Simmons can play both ends of the floor well and handle the ball for their respective teams most of the time but can still finish plays like star big men near the basket. The same can be said of LeBron James, who has been the NBA's premier all-around two-way player over the last decade or so.

With all of that said, any team can benefit from long, mobile, and skilled wings 6'7" or taller because of how they can seemingly play any position in today's pace-and-space era. That is why the Boston Celtics have made it a point to stock up their roster with wings that fit that description. At a glance, it might look like they are top-heavy with versatile and switchable wing players, but it has helped them a lot.

Using their bevy of wing players, the Boston Celtics could play a versatile style of suffocating defense that relies on how they can quickly clog the lane up to prevent driving lanes while still fast enough to recover to open shooters out on the perimeter. There are even moments when they would play three wings simultaneously to provide more mobility and versatility. And among those talented wings, arguably the one with the highest potential is Jayson Tatum.

Standing at least 6'8", Jayson Tatum is tall, long, athletic, and skilled enough to play multiple positions in the NBA. We have seen him dribbling the ball, creating shots, and shooting with ease as a shooting guard does. He has also played his natural position of small forward very well because he can play both inside and outside. And there were even times when he would play the power forward position to help stretch the floor while also defending frontcourt players with similar physical attributes.

While Jayson Tatum's talents and physical gifts are not exactly rare or new in the history of the NBA, he uses them so well that he has become the prototype wing player for any team to have. On offense, his ball-handling, shooting, and finishing abilities allow him to become a very versatile scorer. And on defense, his size, quickness, mobility, and athleticism allow him to switch defensive assignments without losing any productivity as a defender.

Though many other guys in the league can play a similar style, one must consider that Jayson Tatum has so much talent, potential, and work ethic in him. He has become not only a productive player in this modern-day NBA but an All-Star or a superstar in the league. And the scary thing is that he can potentially become one of those Swiss army knife stars that can do virtually anything and everything for his team at a high level.

At such an early stage in his career, Jayson Tatum has indeed shown flashes of what he can potentially do. He was one of the most productive rookies in the NBA during the 2017-18 season, even though he was a part of a particularly deep Boston Celtics team that relied on a more balanced style of offense. When Gordon Hayward went down with an injury early that season, he stepped up big and filled the veteran All-Star's large shoes.

When their best scorer Kyrie Irving was ruled out of the rest of the season later in 2018, Tatum emerged as arguably the Celtics' best wing player. There were even moments when he looked like a veteran star for the Celtics as he was playing at a level higher and more mature than what you would expect from a 20-year-old youngster. And after averaging about 14 points during the regular season, he emerged as the Celtics' top offensive option. He averaged 18.5 points during the playoffs in the absence of Boston's two injured All-Stars.

As the most productive scorer of the Boston Celtics during the 2018 playoffs, Jayson Tatum did not look like a rookie. He fought tooth and nail against some of the Eastern Conference's top wings and guards. And during the 2018 Eastern Conference Finals, he performed admirably against LeBron James himself. At one point, he even dunked the ball hard over James.

Since then, Jayson Tatum has only improved and developed in all facets of the game after patterning his style to childhood idol Kobe Bryant's way of playing the game. Even though Bryant was a Laker for life while Tatum is a Celtic, they did not let the franchise rivalry get in the way of greatness helping another future great. And the work he put himself through in the following years transformed him into a legitimate superstar that can explode for 50 points in a playoff game.

The 60 points he scored against the Spurs in 2021 eventually made people realize just how gifted of a scorer Jayson Tatum is. Following that, when he scored 50 in a win over the Brooklyn Nets in the playoffs that same year, Tatum's star was at its peak. And at only 23 years old, it was scary how much more he could improve as he reached his prime.

As one of the greatest young players the league has in today's era, Jayson Tatum has a chance to carry his team and the NBA on his shoulders in the years to come. He is the proof that the NBA is in good hands, especially when you consider how he and all of the other young greats in the league have been working hard to improve their game. And like his childhood idol, Tatum might even end up winning an MVP and a championship later on in his career.

Chapter 1: Childhood and Early Life

Jayson Christopher Tatum was born on March 3, 1998, in St. Louis, Missouri, to parents Justin Tatum and Brandy Cole. Jayson's parents were never married, and Cole raised him as a single mother. But Justin Tatum was always seemingly around the child's life and often checked up on him while the mother and son lived together.

Brandy Cole was 18 years old when she found out she was pregnant with Jayson. At that time, she was on her way to college but never thought about dropping out. She was pregnant during the majority of her freshman year in college. She then had Jayson during spring break. And after delivering the healthy boy, she went back to class.[i]

However, Brandy brought Jayson with her to classes. As a toddler, the young Tatum attended classes with his mom because no other person could take care of him back home. Even after her undergraduate studies,

Brandy kept studying. She went to business school and eventually law school as well.[i] And the entire time, the young Jayson was there with her.

The mother and son duo did not spend their earlier years together in the most comfortable of situations. Brandy had to juggle time as a student and as a responsible mother, and there were moments when the family had nothing. They had already moved out of Brandy's parents' house when Jayson was just six years old because the mother wanted a life together with her son. But things were never easy for them.[i]

Brandy Cole bought a two-bedroom home for the two of them in the hopes of beating the poverty statistics about teenage single mothers. She worked hard for her education, but things still were not easy for the family. There were bills left unpaid, utilities cut off, and no furniture to enjoy in the house. Jayson Tatum and his mother had to share a bed because they could not afford a second one.

But Brandy kept dreaming and working hard for her son. She supported herself through law school in the hopes of providing a better future for Jayson Tatum. And all that time, the young Tatum was there as a witness to her hardships. He saw how she had to go through thick law books. And the one thing he said to his mom was that he never wanted to be someone who had to read those books.[i] So that was when he dreamed of what was seemingly an impossible goal for him.

When Jayson Tatum was in first grade, his teacher asked him what he wanted to become in the future. In what seemed like a prophetic statement from the young boy, he said that he wanted to become an NBA player. However, the teacher told him to change his dream into something she thought was more realistic. This caused Brandy to confront the teacher to say that she had no right to tell the young Jayson what he could not achieve. After all, Brandy herself was the perfect picture of what pursuing your dreams meant.

Knowing that he had a dream to accomplish and using his mom as his role model in life to pursue what others were saying was an impossible goal for him, Jayson Tatum worked harder than anyone else. As early as 5:30 in the morning, he would tell his mom that he was going out to train. He was so hardworking that he even surprised his father.

Justin Tatum himself was no slouch as a basketball player. The 6'7" forward played bigger than he was and was a productive player for Saint Louis University for three years. He even helped that team win the conference championship in 2000. In the three years he spent with Saint Louis, he averaged 8.2 points and 5.3 rebounds.

During his days in Saint Louis, Justin Tatum often brought his son with him. That was Jayson's first brush with basketball, and he fell in love with it just by watching his father perform well for his team. After Saint Louis, Justin pursued a career overseas as a professional basketball player. During that time, he still managed to support his son and checked up on him frequently.

Because of Justin's influence on Jayson, the young boy started playing basketball. When he was only three years old, he played his first game at the local YMCA. After that, he could not stop talking about basketball and always wanted to play it. There were even times when Brandy had to drive him 50 minutes, once in the morning and another time in the afternoon because there were games he wanted to play. He loved playing basketball so much.[ii]

After his career overseas, Justin Tatum landed a job as a coach at Soldan High School in St. Louis. That gave him and Jayson some time to bond as the younger Tatum often practiced and ran with bigger and older high school players.[ii] That showed how much Jayson Tatum loved basketball and how serious he already was to reach greatness in that sport.

Jayson Tatum was already doing stuff on the basketball court that his youth coaches did not even remember teaching him at a young age. He got a lot of attention from the crowd and often left them speechless with the things he was doing. Even Justin and Brandy could not fathom where he learned the stuff he was doing on the court. It was like Jayson Tatum's love for basketball coincided with his natural feel for the game.

Back in 2006, there was even a time when Jayson Tatum was out there in a Cleveland Cavaliers practice eager to meet the NBA players he thought so highly of. In case you did not know, the 21-year-old LeBron James was already playing for the Cavs at that time. One of his teammates was Larry Hughes, who is one of Jayson's godfathers.[iii]

During that practice, Jayson Tatum was lucky enough to have a chance to join the Cavs' shooting sessions. He was out there shooting hoops together with LeBron

James and legitimate NBA players. But nobody thought that Tatum was well on his way to NBA stardom at that time. And 12 years from that day, Tatum and James would meet on the hardwood floor again but in an entirely different setting. But at that point, Jayson Tatum was still in the early stages of his development.

When Jayson Tatum was 13 years old, he had already reached basketball skills far beyond what other kids of his age had. Being the very supportive mother of her young teenager, Brandy wanted the best for his improving and growing son. That prompted her to try to contact renowned basketball trainer Drew Hanlen, who is known for working with players that were either already playing in the NBA or were inevitably going to star in that league.[ii] At that point, Tatum was neither.

Jayson Tatum was just a skinny teenager that Hanlen thought was not ready to take on the basketball training he conducted. He was not advanced enough physically or mentally to handle the strain and understand the concepts of that level of basketball. However, Brandy Cole was a very resilient mother who did everything to give her son the best.

Bradley Beal, who had just finished a good freshman year in Florida and was on his way to the NBA as the third overall pick of the Washington Wizards, is a longtime friend of the Tatum family. Beal's family is also based in St. Louis, Missouri, and lived a few blocks away from the house where Jayson Tatum grew up. Bradley Beal, who is five years Tatum's senior, was preparing for his rookie season with the Wizards with Drew Hanlen.

Brandy asked Bradley if he could vouch for the young boy he always treated like his younger brother in basketball. While Beal had younger brothers, his family was more inclined towards football instead of basketball. As such, he grew up treating Jayson Tatum as his little brother in basketball and knew how good of a player the young St. Louis native already was. He asked Hanlen to give Tatum a chance.[ii]

The first session Drew Hanlen conducted with Jayson Tatum was supposed to be a test to see whether he had what it took to train with him. As such, it was the most challenging part of it all. Hanlen drove Tatum to the ground and was practically forcing the young man to pass out. There were times when Jayson Tatum was even on the floor, looking like he was about to die from exhaustion. But he never stopped.

Growing up, Jayson Tatum idolized Kobe Bryant. He was using Bryant's signature sneakers and was well aware of the stats that the Laker legend was putting up night in and night out. He watched Kobe's games on video and tried to break down how he played at such a high level so that he could imitate what his idol was doing on the court. As early as the fourth grade, Tatum was emulating moves that Kobe Bryant was doing for the Lakers. He even recalled telling his mother that he wanted to be Kobe.[ii]

Other than his scoring prowess and ability to win championships at the highest level, Kobe was known worldwide for his killer mentality and maniacal and obsessive approach when training to become better. The mentality has helped shape younger generations who have seen what Bryant was capable of both on and off the court. Jayson Tatum was one of those young players that sought to be even half as mentally tough as Kobe is. He was a player that inspired him never to give up.

Jayson Tatum also grew up watching how both of his parents never gave up just to give him the best of what life has to offer. As an 11-year-old, he saw how his mother broke down in the middle of the day but still never gave up when they found out their house was about to be foreclosed. He watched how his father never gave up on his dream of playing high-level basketball when he went overseas to play professionally. Such an upbringing has helped him become a young man with the mental toughness of someone ten years his senior.

After that session with Hanlen, Jayson Tatum thought about how there were plenty of times when he could have given up due to severe exhaustion. However, he wanted to be like Kobe. He wanted to be like his parents, who never gave up and went through tooth and nail just to support his basketball aspirations and dream of becoming an NBA player one day. And Hanlen himself saw that there was no quit in this young man, who he thought had the mental fortitude and toughness of Kobe Bryant.[ii] That led him to believe that Tatum has what it took to be a great NBA player. The young 13-year-old passed his test.

Knowing that Jayson Tatum wanted to be like Kobe Bryant even at that tender age, Drew Hanlen taught the young man how to break down the Black Mamba's game. For an entire week, he showed Tatum how to break down and emulate Bryant's jab step. During that time, the whole workout did not involve even one shot. It was all about fundamentals. The two would watch videos of Kobe and Hanlen would make Tatum replicate Bryant's movements over and over again until he got it right.[ii]

But workouts did not just involve studying Kobe Bryant's fundamental moves. Hanlen and Tatum also watched videos of terrific wing players such as Paul George and Carmelo Anthony. They took elements of how George could pull his own perimeter shots off the dribble while watching how Anthony dominated the mid-post. This continued as Tatum tried to hone his fundamental moves. And when Hanlen believed he was ready, he made him play against his other clients.[ii]

At that age, Jayson Tatum was already playing against professional players that were a decade older than him. They kept beating up the young man, but Tatum kept on coming after them. He always kept improving when he came back after getting beaten. It was that mentality that made him such a spectacular high school athlete at Chaminade College Preparatory School.

Chapter 2: High School Career

Jayson Tatum attended Chaminade College Preparatory School in Creve Coeur, Missouri. As a high school student, what made him stand out in basketball was his sheer determination and hunger to become the best player he could be. As early as 5:30 in the morning, he would be on his way to the gym to train for about an hour just before his classes started.

It was this dedication to basketball that made Jayson Tatum such a sensational high school freshman. In just his first year in high school, he averaged 13.3 points and 6.4 rebounds. He was named Co-Player of the Year and was one of the players responsible for the two championships that his high school team won in 2013.

Then, as a sophomore, he elevated his game and took it to an entirely different level. At just 16 years old in 2014, Jayson Tatum was averaging 26 points and 11 rebounds for the Chaminade Red Devils. He was quickly becoming a nationwide prep sensation and was getting a lot of attention from different universities and colleges.

During his junior season, Jayson Tatum began to show the nation the complete package of his all-around skills. Standing at least 6'8", he had already reached his mature height, but his game was still growing as he continued to dominate the playing field in Missouri. That season, Tatum averaged 25.9 points, 11.7 rebounds, and 3.4 assists.

As good as he was during his junior year, Jayson Tatum had already made believers out of a lot of people in St. Louis. A lot of those were guys that had seen two St. Louis NBA products, David Lee and Bradley Beal when they were still in their formative years as NBA players. And some witnesses already thought that Tatum was just as complete of a player as Lee and Beal.

Gary Lee, David Lee's father and a man supporting the Chaminade basketball program, even said that Jayson Tatum was already just as good as his son and the recently drafted Bradley Beal.[iv] Both David Lee and Bradley Beal became All-Stars during their respective NBA careers. So comparing Tatum to them meant that the young man already showed a lot of talent and promise as a future NBA player.

At about 6'8", he already had a similar height and length to David Lee. But unlike Lee, he was more of a smooth operator out on the perimeter. He was a taller Bradley Beal in many ways because he could hit jumpers with ease, shoot NBA-range three-pointers, and create space for himself out on the perimeter. And thanks to his training with Drew Hanlen, he was already showing advanced skills and footwork.

He could hit step-back shots and turnarounds like Kobe Bryant. When he got to the lane, he was not always trying to force baskets but was more of a graceful finisher that displayed an array of floating jumpers. As a playmaker, he showed a lot of unselfishness and could make the right passes at the right time. He even defended well and was not showing any glaring weaknesses on the court.

Jayson Tatum proved that he was the real deal among juniors during summer 2015 when he went on to play for the St. Louis Eagles of the AAU in the Nike Elite Youth Basketball League. One of his best performances during that tournament was when he made the game-winning shot against Team CP3. He had 28 points to advance to the championship game of that tournament.

And in the tournament finals, Jayson Tatum had 24 points, seven rebounds, and four blocks against the Georgia Stars. However, they ended up losing that game. Nevertheless, Tatum was a monster the entire circuit after putting up 26.5 points and 9.5 rebounds. His performance in the EYBL earned him the attention of many college programs that were more than willing to bring him in. At that time, *ESPN* ranked him as the number two recruit of the high school class of 2016. He was second to Harry Giles, who he defeated in the EYBL.

As the second-best player in his high school class, he naturally drew attention from big-name college programs. Among those programs, Kentucky stood out because of the program's recent track record for developing future NBA All-Stars. Saint Louis, his father's alma mater, was also in the running for the services of the region's best player.

However, Jayson Tatum eventually chose Duke University as his college destination. The primary reason for this was that he thought Duke coach Mike Krzyzewski did the best job at recruiting him and that he saw how Duke and its coaching staff made him their priority. He also loved how Coach K interacted with his players and saw how passionate the legendary coach was at making sure he got the most out of his stars.[v]

As Jayson Tatum was well on his way to a promising college career at Duke, he never forgot about his senior year with Chaminade. He led his team to another state championship that year. And always the very competitive young star, Jayson Tatum's best performances that year were against future NBA players. He had 40 points and 17 rebounds against Malik Monk's Bentonville High School. Then, against Huntington Prep and Miles Bridges, he finished with 46 points. Finally, in a win over popular basketball program DeMatha Catholic School, he had 40 points over Markelle Fultz.

During his senior year, Jayson Tatum averaged 29.6 points and 9.1 rebounds. He had a total of six 40-point games that year and was a participant in the 2016 McDonald's All-American Game. He also participated in the Nike Hoops Summit and was named the National Player of the Year for 2016 over Harry Giles, Markelle Fultz, Josh Jackson, and Lonzo Ball. He ended up with the most points and rebounds in Chaminade history.

After winning the state title that season, Jayson Tatum obsessively played basketball and did his usual training regimen every morning. This even got his mother concerned about the long-term health of her son. Jayson had developed knee tendinitis as early as 14 because he always pushed his body to its limits. As such, she told him to rest his body. Even his high school coaches were telling him to take a break.[ii]

But in his mind, he always thought about Kobe Bryant. There was never a moment when Bryant rested because he never had a plan B or backup plan. Jayson Tatum was a lot like that. He never wanted to be just an NBA player. He wanted to be a star like Kobe Bryant. To that end, he always made sure that he worked his body off like there was no backup plan. For him, it was stardom or nothing. And such a mindset was what helped make him one of the most successful freshmen in his lone season at Duke.

Chapter 3: College Career

Coming into Duke, Jayson Tatum seemed like a jackpot for Coach K and the rest of the Blue Devils coaching staff. Tatum was considered a five-star prospect heading into his freshman year. He was ranked third overall in his recruitment class by both *ESPN* and *Rivals. Scout Media* ranked him fourth overall. He was also considered the second-best small forward behind top-ranked incoming freshman Josh Jackson.

But Jayson Tatum was not the only gem that the Blue Devils got. Duke was always known to be a powerhouse in the college recruitment game. They also acquired big man Harry Giles, who was ranked second overall in his recruitment class by *ESPN*. The other highly-touted incoming freshmen were Marques Bolden and Frank Jackson, ranked 11th and 14th, respectively. Duke was on its way to a season with a roster jam-packed with a lot of talent and potential.

Duke had other talented freshmen joining them and veterans Luke Kennard, Grayson Allen, and Amile Jefferson reprising their roles as the calming figures on that Blue Devils squad. But Jayson Tatum still ended up as arguably Duke's best player that season.

Duke missed Jayson Tatum's services in the first eight games of the season because he was out with a foot injury that he suffered before the beginning of that year's campaign. He made his season debut on December 3, 2016, against Maine. Tatum finished that game with ten points and eight rebounds but was still clearly adjusting after shooting poorly from the field.

His coming-out party was on December 6 in a nationally-televised game against Florida. It seemed as if Jayson Tatum did not feel the pressure of having the entire nation watching what he is capable of when he put up 22 points and eight rebounds in that win for Duke. Since then, Tatum continued to be aggressive as he went on a double-digit scoring streak through his first 12 games that season.

Jayson Tatum scored 20 or more points two more times during that run after that incredible game against Florida. He had 22 points, six rebounds, three assists, four steals, and two blocks in a win over Boston College on January 7, 2017. Then, three days later, in a win over Florida State, he finished with 21 points and four rebounds for the Duke Blue Devils.

On January 30, Jayson Tatum had his first double-double game in college. In that win over Notre Dame, he had 19 points, 14 rebounds, two assists, one steal, and one block. Then, a little over two weeks later, he went on to explode for his highest-scoring game in college. In that win over Virginia, Jayson Tatum finished with 28 points on 8 out of 13 shooting from the field.

In that game against Virginia, Jayson Tatum only had seven points in the first half before Coach K came to him as the two shared the most memorable moment in the young Duke Blue Devil's college career. The legendary coach was livid after seeing that Tatum was too tentative with his shot selection and passed up shots he would have made any other day. Coach K threw his jacket on Tatum's feet and said just a few words that were already enough to fire him up. "You're acting like a soft St. Louis kid," Coach K said.[vi]

After growing up playing basketball, Jayson Tatum was always proud of his St. Louis roots. There are not many good players from that area, and people around the country know that basketball talent is scarce in St. Louis. Whenever Tatum was participating in basketball camps around the country, the one thing his fellow campers always asked him jokingly was if people in St. Louis played basketball.[ii]

Jayson Tatum always took pride in being from St. Louis. His family and friends were from there, he went to school there, and his favorite pizza joint was even there. Anywhere he went, he always made it a point to let people know that he is from St. Louis and that there is a future NBA star that grew up there.

As such, Coach K's words lit a fire in him. He did not want to be that soft St. Louis kid. He wanted to be the greatest player that came from St. Louis. Coach K knew that and wanted to push his best player's buttons.[vi] The result was that Jayson Tatum scored 21 points in the second half of that crucial game against a nationally-ranked team. The 28 points he scored against Virginia were his career-best in points as a college player.

Jayson Tatum was instrumental for Duke in their Conference Tournament win. In the first game against Clemson on March 8, he had 20 points. He followed that up with a win over Louisville with 25 points. Then, in a win over UNC to help Duke qualify for the Conference Championship, he had 24 points and seven rebounds. In the championship-clinching game against Notre Dame, Jayson Tatum finished with 19 points and eight rebounds.

It was difficult to deny that Jayson Tatum was the best player for Duke during that ACC Tournament Championship run. He averaged 22 points, 7.5 rebounds, 2.3 assists, and 1.5 steals during that four-game tournament while shooting 55.4% from the field. Jayson Tatum was named to the All-ACC Tournament team after that fantastic tournament performance from the young 19-year-old from St. Louis.

After winning the ACC Championship, the Duke Blue Devils qualified for the NCAA Tournament as a second seed in the East Regionals. In their first game, which was against Troy, Jayson Tatum finished with his third double-double of the season after going for 18 points, 12 rebounds, four steals, and four blocks. In the second round of March Madness, Duke bowed out of the NCAA Tournament in a loss to South Carolina. In that final college game for Jayson Tatum, he had 15 points.

After what was a great freshman year for Jayson Tatum, he averaged impressive numbers of 16.8 points, 7.3 rebounds, 2.1 assists, 1.3 steals, and 1.1 blocks. He was named to the ACC All-Freshman team and was a member of the All-ACC third team. Tatum finished second behind sophomore wing Luke Kennard in scoring for Duke. He also finished second in the team concerning rebounds. From an overall standpoint, he was arguably Duke's most productive player that season and was undoubtedly one of the more talented freshmen in the nation.

On March 22, 2017, Jayson Tatum announced that he would enter that year's NBA draft as a one-and-done prospect from Duke University. As such, his college career at Duke came to a quick close. But that one single season in college was already enough to make him one of the best players entering the 2017 NBA Draft. He was projected as a player that could be taken in the top five of the draft.

Chapter 4: NBA Career

Getting Drafted

The 2017 NBA Draft was one of the deepest draft classes concerning raw talent and potential. Many big names stood out in that draft class, and some of the teams that were set to pick early in the draft were still undecided on who the best player of the class of 2017 was. Of course, Jayson Tatum's name was in the mix as one of the top players of that year's draft class.

There were a lot of things to like about Jayson Tatum. Physically, he already looked like he was built to play the wing position in the NBA. He already stood 6'8" back when he was a high school junior and was closer to 6'9" when he had his shoes on. He also has a 6'11" wingspan. His shoulders are also broad enough that it looks like he can still put on a few pounds of lean muscle mass.[vii] He may not have been a physical specimen, but Tatum had the right size and length for a wing player in the NBA.

On top of those good physical attributes, Jayson Tatum plays with a lot of fluidity and athleticism at his position. He may be tall and long, but he moves more like a guard when he is out there on the floor. This allows him to play the perimeter wing position well. The same attributes also allow him to become a good option during transition plays.

Offensively, Jayson Tatum knows how to use his physical abilities to his advantage. As a small forward at Duke, he used his long strides to get from point A to point B in a hurry, especially during transition plays.[viii]

There were also stretches where Coach K played him at the power forward position when playing small-ball basketball. In such instances, he could use his speed and length to his advantage to create mismatches against slower big men.

As a scorer, Jayson Tatum was already as polished as anyone can be. The 19-year-old showed promise as a great isolation scorer in half-court sets. He went into the draft as a three-level scorer that could score from the perimeter, shoot from the three-point line, and get to the basket to finish strong with layups and dunks.

When left alone on an island with the ball in his hands, Jayson Tatum's early training as an isolation scorer and his studies and observations of the moves of some of the best isolation wings in the NBA such as Bryant, George, and Anthony allowed him to develop his own identity when left to score the basket on his own. He knows how to use his feet, ball-handling abilities, and quick first step to create space and separation for midrange jumpers. And because of his high release point, Tatum is a challenging cover for any defender when he sees enough daylight to shoot his fluid midrange shots.

There were times when Jayson Tatum looked like a hybrid of Kobe and Melo when trying to score on isolation plays. He knows how to use his jab step to confuse defenders. He is effective at using crossovers and in-and-out dribbles to get his man off-balanced enough to create space for his shots. And when he has the opportunity to do so, he establishes enough separation from the perimeter using fadeaway and turnaround jumpers.[vii]

Using one or two dribbles from the perimeter, Jayson Tatum also showed a lot of potential as a scorer off the dribble. His specialty is when he is going left, and he uses the rhythm of his dribbles to create room and separation for his jumpers. This was his bread and butter back in college as 40% of the shots the nontransition shots that he took came off perimeter two-pointers.[vii]

At his size and length, he has the scoring skills of a shooting guard. That made him a mismatch in college and high school. When they placed a quick and skilled defender on him, Tatum was too tall and long for them to cover his shot. And when teams used bigger but slower defenders, he had enough speed and ball-handling skills to blow by them.

Jayson Tatum also showed his ability to score from the mid-post area, especially when he was up against smaller defenders. He can use his jab step to get his defenders thinking and play with his back to the basket to get closer to the rim or shoot fading jumpers over his defenders. And whenever he was on the low block, he used the same superb perimeter footwork to his advantage by using drop steps and counter moves to create openings under the basket.

One of the deficiencies most college scouts thought Jayson Tatum had coming into his first season with Duke was his lack of consistency as a spot-up threat from beyond the three-point line. However, after making 34% of his three-pointers back in college, it was evident that Tatum was steadily eliminating that weakness in his game and was becoming more of a perfect three-tooled player from the perimeter.

Putting Jayson Tatum on the foul line also was never a good option for any defense. He converted about 85% of his attempts from the free-throw line back in college as he uses the same fluid jump shot mechanics in his free throws. His ability to convert from the foul line made him arguably the most complete scorer in the upcoming NBA draft.

Jayson Tatum already had decent ball-handling abilities that allowed him to handle the ball out on the perimeter when left on an island against his defender. He was not the best dribbler, but his skills were already enough to create space and separation for himself. And although he was not the best playmaker coming into the NBA draft, he was always a willing passer whenever he saw a chance. He showed his quality as a good passer during transition plays.

Rebounding-wise, Jayson Tatum was always good at collecting misses, even when he was a double-double threat back in high school. In college, he was Duke's second-best rebounder. He was a very dangerous player whenever he collected defensive rebounds as a stretch power forward because he could bring the ball up the floor himself and finish strong in transition.

On the defensive end, Jayson Tatum's physical tools should be enough to make him a respectable defender at the NBA level. He has the foot speed to keep up with shooting guards and small forwards. Meanwhile, his height and length are enough for him to contest and defend shots near the basket. His defensive abilities showed from time to time when he was going for interceptions or when he was near the basket blocking shots.

Tatum could also quickly switch out from the paint to guard players at the perimeter when he was locked in at the defensive end. His strides allowed him to recover rapidly over to the perimeter shooter to chase and contest their jumpers. He can even contain guards from time to time using his length and agility.

However, Jayson Tatum's best attribute as a player was his mentality. He is a hardworking young man that does not just want to be good. Ever since he was a young boy, the goal was to be one of the greatest. Such a mentality rubbed off on his game as he was obsessed with reaching another level of basketball.

Jayson Tatum is also a fierce and hungry competitor. Once you light a fire in him, he competes at a hundred percent every time he can. He is confident in himself and knows well how arrogant of a player he is when it comes to competing against the best in the world.[ii]

However, the arrogance that he has is not something that can derail a team's chances. Instead, it is the type of arrogance that allows him to think that he can be better than his matchup and be better than who he was yesterday.

Playing for Coach K in Duke also helped Tatum's ability to play an organized style of basketball. Though he was Duke's best player, the Blue Devil's system did not revolve around a single player but was predicated on playing in transition and on a more organized style of offense on half-court sets. For all of his abilities as an isolation scorer, Jayson Tatum's experience under Coach K made him a coachable player. In that sense, there was no doubt that he could fit in any system in the NBA.

Nevertheless, there were still some flaws to Jayson Tatum's game. For starters, he lacked the heft and strength needed in the NBA, especially when he will play the power forward position during specific stretches. This lack of stability also meant that he would find it challenging to finish near the basket, especially when there is contact. But there still is optimism since his frame looks like it could handle more muscle mass in the long run.

Aside from that, Jayson Tatum is not the type of athlete that would wow you. He possesses above-average explosiveness and will not amaze you with his jumping abilities. He can dunk the ball hard when given a chance, but he does not jump off the roof. He also cannot outrun most other small forwards at the NBA level. Athletically, he is like a slightly quicker and more explosive version of Paul Pierce. In that sense, he is better off using his skills and ability to create separation to score instead of relying on his athleticism.

Though Tatum was regarded as the most complete scorer of his draft class, he still had a few chinks in his armor. His shooting form was already mechanically refined, but he still needed to be more consistent, especially when shooting long-range jump shots. He was used mainly by Duke to bail them out during broken plays, but he still relied more on shooting contested jumpers rather than getting higher quality shots. In that sense, Jayson Tatum tended to settle for ill-advised shots when allowed to isolate his defender. He needed to become a better ball-handler if he wanted to create better shot opportunities for himself.

Jayson Tatum grew up having the ball in his hands a lot of the time because of his ability to score. He was not as adept a scorer when shooting off the catch compared to when he is shooting the ball off a dribble. There were many times when he would rush his shot mechanics out of fear of getting bothered by defenders trying to close out on him. In that sense, he needed to become a better shooter off the catch or a better player when scoring off the ball.

As a passer, Jayson Tatum looked like a confusing player. There were moments when he looked like he did not know whether to shoot or pass because his shoot-first mentality was clashing with his high basketball IQ.[vii] Such instances often led to broken plays, ill-advised shots, or passes that clearly should not have been made. However, there is much optimism in that part of his game because of Tatum's vision and high basketball IQ.

Defensively, Jayson Tatum often looked like he was just going through the motions. He does have the physical tools and the competitive drive to become a great defender, but his efforts on that end of the floor seemed rare. He did not always take the challenge of trying to lock his man down and was easily pushed down on the low block because of his lack of upper and lower body strength.[viii] In that sense, Tatum was still a work in progress on the defensive end. However, there was still a lot of optimism because of his hardworking mentality and physical tools to become a respectable defender in the NBA.

Overall, there was a lot to like about Jayson Tatum's game. However, questions still surrounded his ability to become a productive scorer off the bat in the NBA because of how much better, smarter, bigger, and stronger perimeter wing defenders are at that level of basketball.

There was no denying that Tatum had a lot of talent and potential. Some even regarded him as the best pure scorer in his draft class, and some thought he had the most talent. In that sense, Jayson Tatum needed to be drafted by a team that was unafraid to hone his scoring prowess and willing to wait on him to adjust his scoring skills to the competition he would be facing in the NBA.

As such, although Jayson Tatum was regarded as a top-five prospect, almost nobody thought he would be taken first or second overall in the 2017 NBA Draft.

Instead, people talked about who was better between point guards, Markelle Fultz and Lonzo Ball. However, most scouts and experts thought that Fultz was the safer pick at the top overall spot and would be the most productive player in his draft class off the bat.

Heading into the 2017 NBA Draft, the Boston Celtics owned the top overall pick because they traded with the Brooklyn Nets several years back. As such, they were in the best position to draft Markelle Fultz, who was regarded as the best player of his class coming out of college. But the problem was that the Celtics already had an All-Star point guard in Isaiah Thomas, who was still in Boston at that time and was just coming off his best season as an NBA player.

Knowing that it would have been a wrong decision on their part if they did not choose to draft Markelle Fultz with the top overall pick, the Boston Celtics needed to trade down instead of up. They found a suitable trading partner in the Philadelphia 76ers, who needed a legitimate point guard to share the ball-handling duties with their incoming rookie Ben Simmons. With that, the Celtics traded their top overall pick for the Sixers' third overall pick and a future first-round pick.

On the night of the 2017 NBA Draft, the Sixers drafted Fultz while the Lakers drafted Ball with their second overall pick. The Celtics were then left in the hot seat to choose the best available player left on the board. They needed a wing scorer to help take the scoring load off their All-Star point guard. The most obvious choice was Jayson Tatum.

Some did not think that Jayson Tatum was the best choice for the Celtics. As good of a scorer as Tatum already was at that point in his career, there were fears that he might turn into a Carmelo Anthony in the sense that he would slow down what was known to be a pace-and-space style of offense for the Boston Celtics. Was Tatum going to be a player that would seek isolation baskets for himself instead of playing within the system?

Luckily for Tatum, he landed on a team with a coach known for maximizing his players' best attributes while minimizing weaknesses. A year ago, Brad Stevens led the Boston Celtics to the best record in the East with 5'9" point guard Isaiah Thomas as his best player. He did so by hiding Thomas's defensive weaknesses and putting him in the best situations to utilize his scoring prowess. In that sense, Jayson Tatum could very well be placed in a position that could allow him to make use of his three-level scoring abilities without having to play isolation basketball every time.

Whatever his future with the Boston Celtics was at that time, the important thing was that Jayson Tatum finally made it to the NBA, where he could reach his ultimate goal of becoming one of the greats in the game. He might not have been deemed the best player of his draft class on the night of the draft, but in hindsight, he ultimately turned out to be the better pick compared to both Markelle Fultz and Lonzo Ball after two years in the NBA.

But that was left for the future to show. As of that moment in time, Jayson Tatum was out to show the world that he was a star on the rise. And the best part was that he was only going to make a good team even better than they already were. The Boston Celtics made the right decision and secured their future for years by choosing to go with Jayson Tatum.

Rookie Season, Playoff Debut

When the Boston Celtics drafted Jayson Tatum with the third overall pick, there was a consensus belief that he would be the team's best scoring small forward. It was speculated that he would get a lot of minutes at that position behind other wings, such as Jaylen Brown and Jae Crowder, who was still with the Celtics at that time. However, the team made a drastic change in the months following the conclusion of the 2017 NBA Draft.

During the offseason, the Boston Celtics acquired the services of All-Star small forward Gordon Hayward after he left the Utah Jazz during the free agency period. Hayward played under Brad Stevens in Butler for two seasons in college and has become a better-rounded player at the wing position. There was no doubt that he was going to be their top option at small forward. As such, Tatum was pushed further back in the rotation with the addition of the All-Star forward.

However, a few weeks after acquiring Hayward, the Boston Celtics made another sudden move. Kyrie Irving, who wanted to move from Cleveland and be the secondary option to LeBron James, was looking to become the star of his own team elsewhere. The Celtics acquired him by trading top scorer Isaiah Thomas and Jae Crowder. With Crowder gone, Tatum had the opportunity to fill in the gap left by the forward.

Jayson Tatum proved that he would be a valuable player for the Boston Celtics by dominating the Summer League in Utah and Las Vegas. In the games held in Utah, he averaged astounding numbers of 18.7 points, 9.7 rebounds, and 2.3 steals. Then in Las Vegas, he averaged 17.7 points and eight rebounds. As such, he was named to the All-Sumer League Second Team after performing well against NBA-level competition.

His stint in the NBA Summer League gave him confidence and also placed him on his coach's good side. After seeing Jayson Tatum perform during the Summer League, Brad Stevens realized that this young rookie knew how to play the game and to put the ball through the hoop. He also saw how Tatum drastically improved on the defensive end and put more effort as a defender.[ix]

Nevertheless, Stevens also saw how Jayson Tatum had a few eye-opening moments that made the young rookie realize that he still needed to improve his game a lot.[ix] That said, Stevens was impressed and would give his rookie the minutes he needed to get the confidence essential for a scorer of his caliber in the NBA.

Surprisingly, Brad Stevens thought that Jayson Tatum could be an essential part of the team when playing the small-ball style that was very effective for the Celtics in the previous season when they put the 6'6" Jae Crowder at the power forward spot. In that sense, he thought Tatum's switchability on the defensive end and his ability to stretch the floor and create mismatches for opposing big men could give the Celtics the pacing and spacing they needed to run their style, especially with terrific isolation scorer Kyrie Irving handling the point.

To that end, Jayson Tatum started as the Boston Celtics' power forward in his debut game on October 17, 2017. They were up against the Cleveland Cavaliers and LeBron James, who Tatum met about 11 years back when his eight-year-old self-visited the Cavs' practice facility. In his first NBA game, Tatum finished with a double-double performance of 14 points and ten rebounds.

The Boston Celtics lost that game after suffering an early setback. An early alley-oop play for Gordon Hayward did not go as planned as the All-Star forward ended up breaking his ankle in the worst possible way after landing awkwardly. He never returned that game and the entire season as the Celtics had just lost arguably their second-best player that year. But that was when Tatum stepped up big time and filled the shoes of the All-Star forward. He tried his best to defend LeBron James in that game and his capabilities as a scorer though he still got outplayed by the man regarded as the league's best player.

Though Gordon Hayward was a significant loss for the Celtics that season, they were lucky enough to have drafted the best rookie small forward. With Hayward gone and recovering from his injury, Tatum returned to his natural position of small forward and began playing that role well. He was the perfect player to fill in the shoes left by the All-Star wing.

In a win over the Philadelphia 76ers on October 20, Jayson Tatum had a new career-high in points. He finished that game with 15 points, eight rebounds, and three blocks. Just four days after that, he went on to eclipse his career-high by making 9 of his 15 shots and 4 of 6 three-pointers in a win over the New York Knicks. Tatum finished that game with 22 points, four rebounds, and four steals.

On October 28, Jayson Tatum scored at least 20 points for the second time in his career. He had 20 after shooting an efficient 6 out of 9 from the field and a perfect 2 out of 2 from the three-point line in a win over the Miami Heat. Then, on November 6, he had another 20-point game when he finished a win over the Atlanta Hawks with 21 points and eight rebounds.

Jayson Tatum was one of the catalysts for that hot start for the Boston Celtics that season. After starting their campaign with two losses, they went on to win 17 of the next 18 and on a 16-game winning streak to go 17-3 in their first 20 games. During that run, Tatum proved himself capable enough to handle the scoring load left by Hayward as he averaged 14 points and 5.7 rebounds while shooting 49.7% from the field.

On December 6, Jayson Tatum had his second career double-double after winning over the Dallas Mavericks with 17 points and ten rebounds. And just two nights after that game, he scored 20 points in a loss to the San Antonio Spurs. Tatum shot 6 out of 11 in that game and also collected eight rebounds in the process.

Tatum had the third double-double game of his rookie season on December 16 in a win over the Memphis Grizzlies. He had 19 points and ten rebounds in arguably his best performance as a rookie at that point in his career. He followed that performance up by scoring consecutively in double digits in the next seven games. Tatum averaged 16.6 points and 5.6 rebounds while shooting a ridiculously efficient 55.3% from the field during that eight-game run.

On February 2, Jayson Tatum had his best scoring output at that point of the season. By scoring 27 points in that win over the Atlanta Hawks, he achieved a new career-high in points. He did most of his damage from mid-range in that game after going for 11 out of 19 from the field without making a single three-pointer. He also added four steals to his name in that game.

Jayson Tatum's consistent contribution to a winning Boston Celtics team, who were at the top of the Eastern Conference standings all season long, was enough for him to be named a participant of the Rising Stars Challenge during the 2018 All-Star festivities. As a member of Team USA in that game, he contributed 15 points off the bench but lost to Team World.

After the All-Star break, Jayson Tatum began to take on a more prominent role on the team after the Boston Celtics found out that their best player Kyrie Irving would not return for the remainder of the season due to injury. After only scoring 20 or more points a handful of times during the first half of the season, Tatum went on to have five games of scoring at least 20 points. His best one was when the Boston Celtics beat the Oklahoma City Thunder on March 20. Tatum had his best output as a rookie in that game by finishing with 23 points, 11 rebounds, and four assists.

In the 21 games that Jayson Tatum played after the All-Star break, he averaged 15 points. His final 11 games for the Boston Celtics during the regular season were his best. He averaged 17.5 points on 50.7%

shooting from the floor during that run. It was during those 11 games when he scored 20 or more points five times. After all, he had to take on a bigger scoring load when Kyrie Irving went down with an injury.

Jayson Tatum averaged 13.9 points, five rebounds, and one steal at the end of the regular season. He shot 47.5% from the floor and 43.4% from the three-point line. For a player that shot the majority of his attempts from ten feet and beyond, Jayson Tatum's field goal shooting numbers were pretty impressive as he took advantage of the Boston Celtics' spacing and ball movement. More importantly, Tatum helped the Celtics win 55 games during the regular season to secure the top seed in the East.

If we take Jayson Tatum's rookie numbers merely at face value, they do not seem too impressive at all. However, one must also consider many factors when looking at Tatum's statistics in his first year in the league. He was behind only Kyrie Irving and Jaylen

Brown regarding scoring for that team. Moreover, the Boston Celtics' system was predicated on ball movement, floor spacing, and sharing shots. That was why seven players on the roster averaged double-digit scoring.

Also, we have to consider that the Celtics also played with one of the slowest paces in the league. They were 22nd regarding pacing and 20th overall in points scored per game. As good of an offensive team as they were, the Celtics were even better on the defensive end as they tried to control the game's tempo to allow their players to play a physical brand of defense. So, if you look at it, being able to score 14 points out of the 104 points your team scores on a nightly basis is already impressive, especially if you consider that Tatum was only a rookie back then.

As good of a rookie during the regular season as he was, Jayson Tatum was even better when the stakes were higher. During his NBA playoffs debut, he began showing signs of stardom in the NBA as he placed the team on his back as arguably their most productive player during the postseason. Performing well during the regular season is one thing, but elevating your game during the playoffs is an entirely different story.

In his first playoff game on April 15, Jayson Tatum was instrumental in their Game 1 win over the Milwaukee Bucks. After finishing the game, the rookie sensation had his first playoff double-double with 19 points, ten rebounds, four assists, and three steals. And though he only had four points in Game 2, it was enough for him to help the Celtics get a 2-0 lead over the Bucks.

After scoring 14 points in a big loss in Game 3, Jayson Tatum went on to explode for 21 points in Game 4 to avoid a series tie. However, not even his new career playoff-high was enough for him to help give the Boston Celtics a 3-1 lead as the series was down to a best-of-three heading back to Boston in Game 5.

Jayson Tatum had a subpar outing in Game 5 after going for only eight points. But his presence was already enough to give the Celtics the series lead back. In Game 6, he eclipsed his playoff-high by going for 22 points on 6 out of 14 shooting from the field. However, the Milwaukee Bucks forced Game 7 with that win. It was in the final game of the series When Jayson Tatum started to come into his own. He scored 20 points and had six rebounds and five assists in that Game 7 win to help his team advance to the second round of the playoffs.

Matching up against the Philadelphia 76ers and leading Rookie of the Year candidate Ben Simmons, Jayson Tatum exploded for his best performance at that point in his career. In that Game 1 win for the Boston Celtics, Tatum finished with 28 points while shooting 8 of his 16 shots and 11 of his 12 free throws. He followed that up with 21 points in Game 2 to help lead the Celtics to a 2-0 lead over the Sixers. Then in Game 3, Jayson Tatum scored 24 points on 11 out of

17 shooting from the field to give his team an insurmountable 3-0 series lead.

After that Game 3 performance, Jayson Tatum became the first rookie in Celtics history to score 20 points in five consecutive playoff games. The great Larry Bird held the previous record of four games. Any time you get mentioned in the same sentence as Larry Bird and break a record held by one of the best players in NBA history, you know you are on your way to stardom.

In Game 4, Tatum continued his scoring explosion and mastery over the Sixers' defense by going for 20 points. But Philadelphia managed to escape with a win to avoid a series sweep at the hands of the Boston Celtics. Nevertheless, the inevitable came when Boston defeated Philadelphia in Game 5 to end the series quickly. Jayson Tatum led the way with 25 points on 8 out of 15 shooting from the field.

Jayson Tatum was at his best during that short five-game series against the Philadelphia 76ers. He never scored under 20 points during that second-round encounter and was seemingly a star ready to rise for the Boston Celtics. He averaged 23.6 points, 3.4 rebounds, and 3.2 assists while shooting a ridiculously efficient clip of 52.6% in those five games.

As good as Tatum was in the second round of the playoffs, the Eastern Conference Finals were going to be an entirely different story, especially because they were set to match up with the defending East champions. The Cleveland Cavaliers, who made their fourth consecutive trip to the Eastern Conference Finals, were the kings of the East, mainly because they had LeBron James on that team.

Facing LeBron James in the most critical series in his entire life meant that Jayson Tatum's meeting with the best player in the world 12 years ago had a deeper meaning. When he first came to the Cleveland Cavaliers' practice facility back in 2006, he was still an eight-year-old kid shooting warm-up jumpers with a younger version of LeBron James. At that time, LeBron did not even think he would be good enough to make it to the NBA.

But in 2018, the story had gone full circle. Jayson Tatum was not only good enough to make it to the NBA but was good enough to carry a playoff team on his back to the Eastern Conference Finals against the man who did not even remember meeting him 12 years ago until just recently. But Jayson Tatum and his team were also good enough to force LeBron James and the Cleveland Cavaliers to the limit in that series.

In Game 1, Jayson Tatum scored 16 points on 6 out of 11 shooting from the field and outplayed LeBron, who finished with only 15 points. The Celtics ended up with a win. Then, in Game 2, though LeBron finished with a ridiculous stat line of 42 points, ten rebounds, and 12 assists, Jayson Tatum had help as the Boston Celtics went on to a quick 2-0 start against the defending East champs.

However, Games 3 and 4 were entirely different. The Cleveland Cavaliers ended up tying the series two wins apiece by winning both of their games on their home floor. Jayson Tatum combined for 35 points in those two losses as he and the Boston Celtics were back to square one coming into Game 5.

In Game 5, Jayson Tatum led all Boston Celtics scores with 24 points to go along with seven rebounds, four assists, and four steals to give his team the series lead once again. In another fine playoff performance from the young 20-year-old sensation, the Celtics were one game away from making the NBA Finals for the first time since 2010.

However, LeBron and the Cavs had other things in mind after tying the series again by winning Game 6. With that Cavaliers win in Game 6, the series was down to a crucial seventh and deciding game where all the chips were on the line, and the big-time players would be out there making big-time plays.

In Game 7, Jayson Tatum proved to the entire world that he was indeed a big-time player. Though he was the youngest member of that team, he competed like a fierce NBA veteran and practically carried the team on his back to give them a fighting chance. He was making all the big plays for the Celtics. The biggest one he had was when he dunked on the face of LeBron James during the 6:40 mark of the fourth quarter to cut his team's deficit to only two points.

After that dunk over LeBron James, who was trying his best to block the shot, Jayson Tatum looked like the fiercest competitor on the floor by bumping into the world's best player and giving out a primal scream that would be remembered for years to come. He finished that game with 24 points and seven rebounds, but his team ended up bowing to the Cleveland Cavaliers.

In that seven-game series against the Cleveland Cavaliers, Jayson Tatum averaged 17.9 points on a

49.5% shooting clip. And during the entire playoff run, he was arguably the Boston Celtics' best player after averaging 18.5 points, 4.4 rebounds, 2.7 assists, and 1.2 steals while shooting 47.1% from the floor in 19 total games. He also joined Kareem Abdul-Jabbar as one of only two rookies to score 20 or more points in ten playoff games.

Even after getting dunked on, bumped, and roared at by Jayson Tatum in Game 7, LeBron James had the best things to say about the young Celtic wing. He said that he loved Tatum's competitive fire, demeanor, and the way he plays basketball. James said that Jayson Tatum was a player built for success and stardom in the NBA.[x]

Again, his numbers will not jump out of the roof if you look at them, but it was Jayson Tatum's fierce competitiveness and willingness to put the team on his back that made him stand out during the 2018 playoffs. He was the team's youngest player, but he looked like a seasoned veteran during the Boston Celtics' incredible run to the Eastern Conference Finals.

Without Kyrie Irving and Gordon Hayward, their two All-Star scorers, the Boston Celtics were not on anyone's radar coming into the postseason because everyone knows that the playoffs are where stars shine the brightest. But it was a 20-year-old rookie who was just fresh off his lone season as a college student one year ago, who shone the brightest for the Boston Celtics. Nobody even thought that Jayson Tatum would be good enough to make an impact as a rookie, but there he was, proving to the world how talented a young star he was at that point in his basketball career.

Although the season may have been over for the Boston Celtics, things were not done for Jayson Tatum. The annual NBA awards show was next shortly after the Golden State Warriors swept the Cleveland Cavaliers in the NBA Finals. Jayson Tatum was selected as one of the three finalists for the 2018

Rookie of the Year award. The other two were Ben Simmons of the Philadelphia 76ers and Donovan Mitchell of the Utah Jazz. Both of those rookies were just as deserving of the award as Tatum was.

The case for Ben Simmons was that he was the NBA's most consistent all-around rookie at that time. The 6'10" Australian point guard was putting up some of the best overall numbers the NBA has ever seen and was racking up triple-doubles while almost singlehandedly changing the culture of a franchise that had been the laughing stock of the NBA over the past handful of seasons before this one. He averaged 15.8 points, 8.1 rebounds, and 8.2 assists for the Sixers that season.

Meanwhile, the electric 6'3" guard Donovan Mitchell also had a strong case for the Rookie of the Year award. The athletic guard who could seemingly jump off the roof turned out to be the most sensational scorer among the rookies after averaging 20.5 points,

3.7 rebounds, and 3.7 assists. Before the draft, he was not even among the biggest names of the class of 2017 and only drafted 13th overall. And above that, some would say that he was a "true rookie" because he was drafted before the season, unlike Ben Simmons, who was drafted in 2016 but had to sit out the 2016-17 season due to injury.

Then we go back to Jayson Tatum, who did not have the most impressive stats but had a season just as remarkable as any other rookie in the league. Tatum did not lead the rookies in any major statistical category and was not even on the top five concerning points per game, even though he was heralded as the most complete scorer out of all the rookies of his draft class.

However, whatever Jayson Tatum lacked in stats, he more than made up for in wins and impact on the floor for the Celtics, especially after Kyrie Irving went down with an injury. You will only appreciate his game if you see him playing live. He has the demeanor of a star and the competitive drive of an all-time great. And he rarely made any glaring mistakes on the floor as he competed as he could on both ends, even as a rookie with no previous NBA experience.

If you factor in his smooth shooting, ability to create shots for himself, his effort as a defender, and the way he contributed to his team all season long to help them win the top seed in the East, Jayson Tatum was just as deserving to be named Rookie of the Year as anyone else. He may not have been the best as far as stats, but he showed a type of talent, consistency, and maturity that were all well beyond his years.

But when the awards show came, Ben Simmons ultimately won the Rookie of the Year award in what was one of the more tightly contested races in recent memory. Jayson Tatum finished third and did not even get a single first-place vote. Nevertheless, his performance during the playoffs defined him as a player and future NBA star instead. At a tender age, he has already gotten deeper into the playoffs than most other seasoned NBA stars. And when you get to taste success, you will always want more of it. That said, Tatum was only going to get better and hungrier as his career progressed.

On the Rise

Though Jayson Tatum was already showing a lot of promise during the 2017-18 season, mainly when he carried the Boston Celtics during that 19-game playoff run to the Conference Finals, there still was much room left for him to grow so that he would become the total package. He may be on the way to stardom, but Tatum still needed to work more on his game if he wanted to become an All-Star quickly.

The first thing that Tatum needed to work on was strength. He is not a skinny or weak athlete, but his power and frame were still lacking compared to the likes of a LeBron James, who he had to defend in certain stretches during the playoffs. And when he wants to be an effective power forward in small-ball situations, he needs to develop his strength more and add a bit of heft to ensure that he would not get pushed around inside the paint.

Playmaking is the second thing he needed to improve on if he wants to develop into a total package at the small forward position. One of the hallmarks of the Boston Celtics' success is their ball movement and ability to find the best possible shots by constantly passing the ball. In that sense, Tatum must develop his ability to make plays for others if he wants to become a more effective player under the Celtics' system. That should be a crucial part of his game if a star goes down with an injury again.

Third, Jayson Tatum needed to be more assertive. The Boston Celtics were still Kyrie Irving's team. He was still the first option on offense and should have more touches than anyone else on the team. But if Kyrie was not on the floor, someone else should learn how to step up and take responsibility as the top option on offense. Jayson Tatum was the best candidate for that job because he is probably the only other player who knows how to manufacture his own shot. In that sense, Tatum needed to become more assertive as an option on offense to turn into a star on the rise.

Defense was also another thing that any player could not focus enough on. In Tatum's case, he was not a defensive liability for the Boston Celtics in his first year with them. Whether that was because of how Brad Stevens hid his lapses on the defensive end or because he made significant strides in that part of his game, it was evident that Jayson Tatum was already a respectable defender when he was just a rookie.

However, the Boston Celtics were heading into the 2018-19 season as a deep team with several players who could take over the scoring responsibilities at any given night. The best way for Jayson Tatum to contribute to his team consistently was to take the defensive load away from their other stars. You can have bad nights on offense, but the Celtics had more than enough weapons to augment possible scoring droughts from Tatum. But the defensive end was something no player in the league can ever slump on.

That said, contributing consistently on the defensive end was more of a mindset for Tatum than a skill. He already had the physical tools and competitive drive to become an elite defender, much like how his childhood hero Kobe Bryant was for most of his legendary career. What Jayson Tatum needed more coming into his second season was to develop that killer defensive mindset that would allow him to own his defensive assignment and make it a point to shut down whoever he was tasked to defend.

Of course, Jayson Tatum also had to work on his skill level to develop into a better-rounded offensive player. As such, he made a childhood dream of his come true by training with none other than his favorite player Kobe Bryant, who was kind enough to agree to train the young man even though the Lakers and the Celtics are the most storied rivals in all of basketball.[xi]

One of the many things that the two worked on during the offseason was footwork. Bryant is legendary when it comes to his footwork. Hakeem Olajuwon and Michael Jordan may be the only ones on par or better than Kobe when it comes to footwork. This part of the game allowed Kobe Bryant to stay an effective player deep into his career, and this was something that Tatum needed to work on to learn how to manufacture better shot attempts from the perimeter. And of course, it also would not hurt if a little bit of that famous "Mamba Mentality" rubbed off on him.

Jayson Tatum also sought the help of another legend. This time, he worked out with Penny Hardaway, one of the best all-around players during the '90s era before injuries sidetracked what could have been a storied career. Known primarily as a large point guard, Hardaway's height and frame at his peak were similar to Tatum's, even though the latter's game was more like Kobe's. However, Tatum trained with Hardaway not to improve his scoring output but to become a better ball-handler and more generous playmaker.[xii]

Those offseason training sessions that Tatum had with two legendary guards would be crucial for him and his team in the upcoming season. Nobody was going to expect him to average 20 points a night for the Celtics because of how deep that roster is and because the system is predicated more on controlling the game's pace while sharing possessions of the ball.

However, it was still crucial for Tatum to become a more efficient scorer because he would have to share possessions with Kyrie Irving and Gordon Hayward. And if he wanted to become a better team player for the Boston Celtics, he also needed to learn how to locate the two All-Stars and pass the ball to them at the right time. In other words, his offseason training was for developing his ability to coexist with the returning stars rather than just making him a complete individual player.

When the regular season started, it appeared that Jayson Tatum had improved a lot throughout the offseason. In his first game of the 2018-19 regular season on October 16, 2018, Tatum finished with 23 points, nine rebounds, and three assists in a win over the Philadelphia 76ers.

But just four days later, he immediately outdid himself by going for 24 points and a career-high of 14 rebounds in a win over the New York Knicks. Jayson Tatum would again score 24 points on October 25 in a win over the Oklahoma City Thunder. He hit 8 of his 18 shots and all seven of his free throws in that game.

After going for 21 points in a loss to the Utah Jazz on November 9, Jayson Tatum scored a new season-high in points two nights later in a loss to the Portland

Trailblazers. He finished that game shooting 9 out of 18 from the floor and 5 out of 9 from the three-point area. And four days after that, he had 21 points and seven rebounds in a win over the Toronto Raptors. Through his first 20 games of the 2018-19 season, Jayson Tatum averaged improved numbers of 16.2 points and 6.6 rebounds.

Jayson Tatum had his second double-double performance on December 12 in a win over the Washington Wizards and his childhood friend Bradley Beal. In that game, he put up 12 points and collected 12 rebounds. Is third double-double game of the season came on Christmas Day when he had 23 points and ten rebounds in another fantastic performance against the Philadelphia 76ers.

On January 14, 2019, Jayson Tatum had the best scoring game of his young career in a loss to the Brooklyn Nets. In the first time he scored at least 30 points in an NBA game, Tatum hit 12 of his 19 shots,

3 of his five three-pointers, and 7 of his 11 free throws to score a new career-high of 34 points. That remained the only time he scored at least 30 points all season long.

Just two days after putting up a new career-high, Jayson Tatum went for another double-double game and his first double-double of the New Year in a win over the Toronto Raptors. He had 16 points and ten rebounds that game. Several weeks later, on February 7, he had an excellent all-around performance in a loss to the Los Angeles Lakers. Tatum finished that game with 22 points, ten rebounds, and five assists. And right before the All-Star break, he had 20 points and ten rebounds in a win over the Philadelphia 76ers.

For a second consecutive year, Jayson Tatum took part in the Rising Stars Challenge as a member of Team USA. This time, however, he was a much better performer than he was a year ago. As a starter, he had 30 points on 12 out of 24 shooting from the field. He was second overall in scoring, and only Kyle Kuzma could edge him out in points in that win for Team USA.

When he returned from the All-Star break, Jayson Tatum put up a double-double performance of 17 points and ten rebounds in a one-point loss to the Milwaukee Bucks. And then, on March 6, he had a sound scoring output of 24 points on 8 out of 17 shooting from the field in a win over the Sacramento Kings.

The next time Jayson Tatum scored 20 or more points was on March 26, when the Boston Celtics defeated the Cleveland Cavaliers. In that game, he finished with 21 points, five rebounds, and four assists. The final time he scored 20 or more points was on April 5, when he had 22 points and seven rebounds in a win over the Indiana Pacers, who they would meet in the first round of the playoffs that year.

At the end of his second year with the Boston Celtics, Jayson Tatum averaged improved numbers of 15.7

points, six rebounds, and 2.1 assists. His role increased as he was second on the team for possessions and shots taken. He was also second only Kyrie Irving in points per game that season as Tatum had developed into the Boston Celtics' secondary option on offense.

Meanwhile, the Boston Celtics struggled quite a bit all season and would only win 49 games after securing the first seed in the last two seasons. They did not live up to expectations that season. Some experts and analysts believed that they would become an even better team with the return of Irving and Hayward and the continued development of youngsters Jayson Tatum and Jaylen Brown.

Some analysts believed that the Boston Celtics failed to live up to expectations because of their problems with chemistry. As good as Kyrie Irving is as a star, he is not an ideal point guard in a system that relies on ball movement. Gordon Hayward was still trying to get back to at least half of the All-Star form he played two seasons ago. As such, the Celtics saw a few bumpy roads along the way that they struggled to get over.

Nevertheless, the team proved that chemistry was not an issue when they got to the playoffs. Because the playoffs are an entirely different monster, the Boston Celtics were free to play their physical brand of defense. And, of course, big-time players like Jayson Tatum come to play better when the stakes are higher. That is why he did in their first-round encounter against the Indiana Pacers.

Though it was more of a team effort, and though Kyrie Irving led the team in scoring in the first round, Jayson Tatum played well against the Pacers as the Celtics swept their opponents out of the playoffs in only four games. Jayson Tatum averaged 19.3 points and 5.5 rebounds in that four-game series while shooting 51% from the field. His best performance came in Game 2 when he had 26 points on 11 out of 20 shooting from the field.

However, the Boston Celtics suddenly looked like the team everyone thought they were—a squad that lacked chemistry among its best players. This became apparent when they faced off against the Milwaukee Bucks, the top team in the Eastern Conference, in the second round. And the chemistry issues became obvious due to the Bucks' suffocating defensive style.

The problem with the Boston Celtics during that series against the Bucks was that they were forced to play hero ball instead of relying on a pace-and-space style with plenty of ball movement. Anyone could credit the Bucks' stifling defense in that series, but you could also point out the fact that the Celtics just did not play the same kind of team-oriented style that they had a year ago when they were moving the ball, sharing possessions, and fighting hard on defense.

With Kyrie Irving, the team's best player at that time, having the ball most of the time, all while the Milwaukee defense was so focused on giving him bad shots, none of the other players on the Celtics could have their opportunities to make plays throughout most of that series. The Celtics may have won Game 1 by 22 points with Kyrie Irving making plays for his teammates, but the Bucks eventually learned to focus on the Boston point guard.

In that regard, Jayson Tatum shot poorly in the first two games as he combined for 4 out of 17 from the field. He had his best game in Game 3, but he failed to get the number of shot attempts that would have helped his team in that loss. Everything became futile as the Celtics lost four straight games following a surprising Game 1 win for them.

Even though Tatum had a respectable performance in the first round, his efficiency and shot attempts went down in the second round against the Milwaukee Bucks. In those five games, he averaged 12 points on a dismal 36.4% shooting from the field. And for a player that was supposed to be the Celtics' future, he only had 11 shot attempts per game against the Bucks.

While fingers began pointing to Kyrie Irving as someone who tried to force his way through that series with his brand of hero ball, what was clear was that the chemistry was problematic, especially when you compare it to the season the Celtics had a year ago. But Irving was not the only one to blame, as Jayson Tatum also had his faults in that series and probably the entire season. That loss to the Bucks made it evident that changes needed to be made during the offseason.

First All-Star Appearance

During the 2019 offseason, the Boston Celtics saw a massive change in the roster when Kyrie Irving decided to leave for the Brooklyn Nets as a free agent to join superstar Kevin Durant on that team. Meanwhile, not to be outdone by the loss of their star point guard, the Celtics acquired All-Star Kemba

Walker to serve as essentially the replacement of Irving.

Plenty of people were surprised by the decision of getting Walker, who was not so different from Irving in terms of his style as a score-first point guard. After all, plenty of people thought that Kyrie Irving's style and personality ruined the Celtics' chemistry both on and off the court. But while Walker may have played a similar style, he had a different character and was more likely to defer to star teammates.

But, of course, while people loved pointing their fingers to Irving when talking about the failed season that the Celtics had a year ago, Tatum himself was not all that innocent. That's because there were also problems when it came to his scoring. As talented as he may be, he was still a young player who needed to learn to become more efficient.

Many people pointed out how Jayson Tatum was seemingly in love with the long two-point shot during his second year in the NBA. Throughout the league's history, the best players in the NBA were always proficient midrange shooters who knew how to create their shots from the perimeter off the dribble. Michael Jordan, who came in as a slasher, eventually learned to hone his midrange shot as he aged. Kobe Bryant did the same when he became a more proficient midrange jump shooter as he matured. Even Kevin Durant and Kawhi Leonard, arguably the best mid-range shooters in the league, also incorporated that shot into their arsenal. In that sense, having an excellent midrange shot allowed a player to become a superstar scorer because he needed to have options whenever the drive and three-point shot were taken away from him.

In the past, the midrange shot was the secondary offensive option that most players went to whenever they did not have any driving lanes. However, in the modern NBA, it became a fallback option that players needed to have in their arsenal if they needed to go to a shot that defenses were more likely to give up. That is why most of the championship teams in the league had someone who could get a long two-pointer at any given moment if opposing defenses were too focused on guarding the extremes, which were the paint and the three-point line.

But the problem when it came to Jayson Tatum during his sophomore campaign in the NBA was that he was seemingly obsessed with becoming similar to Kobe Bryant. Instead of focusing on his drives or three-pointers, the young gun was much more likely to pull up from the midrange, even though it was not the best shot selection at any given moment. As mentioned, the modern NBA demands that you have a midrange shot not as a top priority on offense but as a backup option that you could go to whenever your other options are taken away from you. In Tatum's case, it was his priority to try to go for long two-pointers even though the shot was not there.

The number showed how Tatum favored the two-pointer above all other shots. 70% of his shots came from within the perimeter. Meanwhile, over 30% of those shots came from within ten feet and the three-point line. If we focused on the midrange shots, 27.7% of his total shots were midrange attempts.[xiii] But while shooting midrange jumpers should not be a problem as long as that shot was within the player's arsenal, it becomes a problem when you take too many contested long two-pointers.

In Jayson Tatum's case, he did indeed have the midrange shot in his arsenal, but the numbers also show that his field-goal percentage from within 16 feet and the three-point line was a dismal 35%. That means that he not only took a lot of these shots, but he also struggled to make such shots. This is where the analytics come in because Tatum shot 37.3% from the three-point line that season. So, if he had chosen to take three-pointers instead of dribbling into contested long two-pointers, he would have been a lot more efficient as a scorer, considering that the three-point shot is worth an extra point.

That said, while it was clear that the league's best players needed to have a midrange shot if they wanted to win championships, those shots are still very much the worst shot in basketball from an analytical standpoint. As such, players needed to go for that shot only when it was available to them instead of looking for a long two-pointer just a few feet away from the more efficient three-point shot. In Tatum's case, it was needless to say that his shot selection needed work. He already had the tools to score 20 points at any given moment, but all he needed to do was to know how to use those tools properly.

It also was a problem that Jayson Tatum was not allowed to be himself during the previous year. While he did showcase what he could do as the top offensive option during the 2018 playoffs when Irving was injured, Tatum had to become a secondary offensive option a year ago because he needed to defer to the ball-dominant Kyrie Irving. But if he could have the ball more in his hands and create plays for himself or others, things might change for the better because Tatum was always someone who preferred having possession of the ball. He could still score off the ball, but his identity was that of a ball-dominant scorer.

Of course, if Jayson Tatum needed to improve as a shot-creator when the ball is in his hands, he also needed to improve the tightness of his handles so that defenses could not bother his dribbles whenever he is trying to look for his shot. Doing so will make him a better isolation basketball player rather than just a simple complementary piece to an All-Star player.

As young as Tatum was, he still needed to add more moves to his arsenal because of how it is always essential for a ball-dominant player to know how to create separation from his defender. During his younger years, Kobe Bryant relied more on his ball-handling to create separation but eventually learned to rely on his footwork to create space between him and his defender. And considering that Tatum was a Bryant disciple, learning how to add simple shakes, jab steps, and foot movements could help him create the space he needed to shoot over his defenders.

That said, the Boston Celtics needed Jayson Tatum to become the best player he could be in time for the next season, especially with all of the changes they had in their core. Kemba Walker may have been their best player coming into the season but, if he could grow and learn from his past mistakes, there was no reason why Tatum could earn the status of a franchise player. And that was precisely what he did during the 2019-20 season.

After that sophomore slump from Tatum, he immediately showcased an improved offensive game during the earlier portions of the 2019-20 regular season as the Celtics jumped to a quick 10-1 record through their first 11 games. They may have lost the season opener, but they went on ten consecutive wins after that. And during that 10-game winning streak, Tatum averaged nearly 20 points.

Jayson Tatum also exploded for 30 points twice during the early portion of the season. The first one was in a loss to the LA Clippers on November 20, 2019. Then, on December 1, he scored 30 again but on the New York Knicks. But it was not until December 22 that Jayson Tatum exploded for a new career-high in scoring. In his best performance at that point in the season, he went for 39 points and 12 rebounds in a blowout win over the Charlotte Hornets. From then on, Jayson Tatum just kept getting better and better.

On January 11, 2020, Jayson Tatum went for a new career-high of 41 points in a massive 35-point win over the New Orleans Hornets. He was 16 out of 22 from the field in that win. And the best part was that he only needed to play 30 minutes to dominate the

Pelicans in that fantastic performance from such a young and rising player. He was also quickly becoming the Celtics' best player.

Unfortunately, on January 26, 2020, the NBA received one of the first of much shocking news. It was announced that Kobe Bryant, his second daughter Gigi, and several other passengers were part of a helicopter crash that took all of their lives earlier that day. The news was shocking and heartbreaking to the entire world, considering how beloved Kobe was and how Gigi was looking to become the next big thing in women's basketball. But on Tatum's part, he felt worse because he grew up idolizing Kobe Bryant as the Michael Jordan of his generation.

Following Bryant's death, Tatum posted a photo of himself as a young boy wearing a Lakers jersey while standing side by side with Kobe Bryant. He captioned the photo with:[xiv]

Heartbroken. My Hero. My Idol. The reason I started to play this game, the reason I fell in love with this game. Growing up wanting to be just like you, to you becoming a mentor, beyond thankful for everything you've done for me. "I didn't have a plan B I put all my eggs in one basket and I knew I was going to make it happen" hearing you say that stuck with me every day of my life. You inspired me and I am forever grateful more than you know! Love you Bean □□ ❤□! Sad, sad, sad day RIP Kobe and Gianna! Praying for the family!

A few days after Bryant's death, Jayson Tatum said in an interview that it still hurts to realize that his childhood idol was already gone. He also said a few things about what made him love Kobe Bryant, who was always his favorite player and the man he patterned his game from.

"For me, the thing I fell in love with him about was his work ethic, how he wanted to outwork his potential and outwork everybody and prove that he was the best," Tatum said. "That's exactly what he did"[xv]

For Tatum's part, the next thing he needed to do for himself and Bryant was take his game to the next level. Throughout his entire career, Bryant made sure that he was the best at what he did by working hard on his game and adding new touches to his arsenal every single season until he had to retire due to injuries. That said, Jayson Tatum needed to become his version of a Kobe Bryant if he wanted to be as legendary as his childhood idol. He had the opportunity to do so shortly after the death of his favorite player.

When Kemba Walker missed several games during February, Tatum showcased what he could do as the undisputed top offensive option for the Celtics. Throughout the entire month of February, Jayson Tatum averaged 30.7 points while shooting 49.4% from the field and 48.1% from the three-point line to keep the Celtics afloat in the absence of their All-Star point guard. During that run, he scored 39 points against the Clippers on February 13 before exploding for 41 points against the Lakers in his tribute game for his departed idol.

And speaking of All-Star, Jayson Tatum was selected to participate in the All-Star Game that season as one of the many first-time All-Stars in 2020. This was the first step he needed to take to become as legendary as Kobe Bryant was. Of course, because Tatum was no longer looking to become Bryant 2.0 and was now looking to become his own unique player, being selected as an All-Star was the validation he needed to know that the hard work he put himself through since his rookie year was indeed working.

About three weeks after the All-Star Game, the NBA received another bad news. The Utah Jazz center Rudy Gobert was the first player to test positive for COVID-19, which had already become a global pandemic. Due to how fast COVID-19 spreads and how fatal it can become, the NBA announced on March 11, 2020, that they would be suspending the season indefinitely until they could come up with a solution to combat the effects of the virus on the way games were being played.

After the NBA season was suspended, all of the people involved with the league and the entire country were asked to quarantine themselves at home indefinitely. This meant that the players and coaches were not allowed to meet or do any basketball-related activities as a team. The only way they could play basketball was if they could do individual sessions in private gyms.

During that time, Jayson Tatum took the opportunity to spend more time with his family at home. Like many players, he spent his quarantine days watching shows and movies and doing individual workouts to make sure he was still in great shape if ever the NBA did indeed resume its operations sooner or later. It took almost four months for the league to find a solution that they believed could help continue the season.

In June 2020, the NBA, which included the league's governing body, the coaches, and the players, came up with an answer to the effects of COVID-19 on the 2019-20 season. They announced that they would be restarting the season at the end of July 2020 as 22 teams would be invited to participate in a "bubble" in Orlando, Florida. The 22 teams included the top eight teams from each conference and six other teams within eight games from the eighth seed of their respective conferences.

At that point, the Boston Celtics were one of the top eight teams in the East. It is needless to say that they were invited to take part in the bubble games in Orlando. The format was that they needed to play eight seeding games to decide the positions in the playoffs. Then, after that, the playoffs would proceed in the usual format, but all of the games would be played out in the Orlando bubble.

When the Boston Celtics played their first seeding game in Orlando, it was clear that Jayson Tatum was rusty following nearly five months of not playing competitive basketball. In that game against the top-seeded Milwaukee Bucks on July 31, 2020, Tatum scored only 5 points while shooting 2 out of 18 from the floor. But he needed that game to shake the cobwebs off and to shock his system back to his usual routine before the season's suspension in March.

After that dismal game against the Bucks in his first game in nearly five months, Jayson Tatum did not look rusty when he scored 34 points in a win over the Portland Trailblazers two days later. He eventually continued to shoot and score well from the field while helping the Boston Celtics earn the third seed in the Eastern Conference after the seeding games in Orlando.

At the end of his first-ever All-Star season, Jayson Tatum averaged 23.4 points, seven rebounds, three assists, and 1.4 steals, which were all career-highs for him at that point in his NBA career. He also earned All-NBA Third Team honors as he had risen to become a legitimate star that could perhaps become one of the faces that could lead the league into the future. It was all thanks to his improvement from a year ago.

While many argued that not having Irving allowed Tatum to rise because he was now allowed to have more possessions and shot attempts, you also need to consider that Kemba Walker, a shoot-first point guard, was still around. Tatum's improvement can be attributed to how hard he worked on his game and his overall growth as a shot creator. Let's look at his shooting numbers, shall we?

During the 2019-20 season, Jayson Tatum shot 45% from the field and 40.3% from the three-point line, nearly doubling his three-point shot attempts. In line with how Tatum increased his three-point shots was the decreased volume of his long two-pointers. After attempting 27.7% of his shots from the midrange a year ago, Jayson Tatum reduced that number to 17.9% while increasing his three-point attempt percentage from 29.8% to 37.4%.[xiii]

That meant that, instead of dribbling into long two-pointers that were contested, he learned to embrace the value of the equally challenging but more rewarding three-point shot. And because he still did not disregard the midrange jumper from his game, it became apparent that he was buying into the same style that made the likes of Kevin Durant and Kawhi Leonard superstars. He still incorporated the midrange shot, but not as a forced shot that he needed to go to every play.

Some people can also point out that his usage rate increased that season, which is why his stats increased. Of course, no coach would ever rely on increasing a player's usage rate without seeing an improvement in his shot selection, shot discipline, and decision making. In that sense, Tatum's minor tweaks in his game were more than enough to increase his efficiency alongside his increased usage rate.

But the most impressive part about Tatum's game came from his improved ability to self-create shots. During the 2019-20 season, there was a stark increase in his on-the-ball shot attempts while corresponding with the decrease in his off-the-ball shot attempts. That meant that the Celtics trusted him so much that they were willing to give him the ball and allow him to create plays for himself or others.

The fact that he became more of an isolation shot-creator meant that his handles have improved, and he has put in some moves and shakes that allowed him to create some space between him and his defender. And any scorer knows that an extra inch of separation makes an entire world of difference when it comes to the efficiency of a shot attempt.

Despite how impressive Jayson Tatum's growth was on the offensive end, you can also see a marked improvement from him on the defensive end of the floor. He was one of the leaders on defensive real plus-minus throughout much of the entire regular season, which is one of the best indications of a player's defensive impact when he is on the floor. So, even if he was not getting crazy defensive stats, the fact that he could lock his defensive assignment down and switch onto bigger or smaller players alike allowed him to become arguably the most valuable defender on the Boston Celtics lineup. He was by no means a Kawhi Leonard on defense but being able to defend all positions from point guard to power forward with his versatility made him a valuable defensive asset.

Jayson Tatum's impressive rise on both ends of the floor would only become more critical in their playoff run in the Orlando bubble that year. The Celtics had a legitimate chance at the NBA title or, at the very least, a finalist spot. And the road to another deep playoff run needed to start in the first round against the Philadelphia 76ers.

Using his versatility against a bigger yet slower Philadelphia 76ers team, Jayson Tatum dominated the Celtics' first-round opponents by leading Boston to a four-game sweep. It started when he delivered 32 points and 13 rebounds in Game 1. Following that performance, he finished Game 2 with 33 points on an impressive 8 out of 12 shooting from the three-point line. Jayson Tatum closed the series with 28 points and 15 rebounds to make it to the second round. Tatum averaged 27 points and 9.8 rebounds during that first-round encounter while shooting 48.7% from the field.

In the second round, Jayson Tatum and the Celtics were seemingly on their way to unseating the Toronto Raptors from their throne as the defending NBA champions. In Game 1, Tatum went for 21 points and nine rebounds. Then, in Game 2, he went for a fantastic performance of 34 points, eight rebounds, and six assists to give his team a 2-0 lead.

While the Toronto Raptors tied the series by winning Games 3 and 4, the Celtics won a critical Game 5 thanks to Tatum's 18 points and ten rebounds. And even though the series reached seven games, Tatum was able to punctuate the second-round win for the Boston Celtics with 29 points, 12 rebounds, and seven assists in a fantastic closeout performance for the rising superstar.

Following that series win over the Toronto Raptors, the Boston Celtics were in an excellent position to make it to the NBA Finals if they could beat the Miami Heat in the Eastern Conference Finals. However, after going for 30 points and 14 rebounds in Game 1, the Heat escaped with a win. The same thing happened in Game 2 as Miami grabbed a 2-0 lead.

Escaping a 0-3 hole, Jayson Tatum put his team on his back in Game 3 with a fantastic all-around performance of 25 points, 14 rebounds, and eight assists. Still, Boston fell 1-3 after losing Game 4. Not willing to bow out of the playoffs, Tatum had another fantastic performance after going for 31 points, ten rebounds, and six assists in Game 5. However, Miami eventually made it to the NBA Finals by closing the Boston Celtics out in six games.

Despite failing to make it to the Finals in his second time in the Eastern Conference Finals in three seasons, Jayson Tatum showed up during the 2020 playoffs by averaging superstar numbers of 25.7 points, ten rebounds, and five assists. At this point, it had become apparent that he was already indeed the Boston Celtics' best player and franchise superstar.

Superstardom

Entering the 2020-21 season, which was set to start late in December due to the effects of COVID-19, the

Boston Celtics kept their core players intact and hardly changed the lineup. For some, this looked like it was good news for the Celtics because they were able to get as far as the conference finals a year ago with the same core. However, that was not exactly the case during the entire season when the Celtics struggled with injuries and lineup changes.

In Jayson Tatum's case, he also experienced a few problems during the earlier part of the season despite starting it well enough. Tatum finished the season opener for the Celtics with a game-winning three-pointer over the outstretched arms of the Milwaukee Bucks's Giannis Antetokounmpo. Then, on January 4, 2021, he went for a new season-high of 40 points in a win over the Toronto Raptors.

However, Jayson Tatum had to miss five straight games during January because he tested positive for COVID-19. While Tatum, as healthy as he is, did not experience the same effects that other people do when they contract COVID-19, the virus still did enough damage to him shortly after he recovered from it and finally tested negative.

Coming back from COVID-19, Jayson Tatum was vocal about how he felt like he had trouble breathing due to the effects of the virus.[xvi] While he was still a fantastic player after he recovered from the virus, he felt like he was not the same as far as his stamina was concerned, primarily because of how COVID-19 targets the respiratory system.

That said, Tatum looked inconsistent at times on both ends of the floor. Last season, he was one of the best defensive forwards in the league because of his overall versatility. But, during the 2020-21 season, his defense fell, probably because he had to conserve his stamina for his offense. And with Kemba Walker missing a lot of games that season, it was important for Tatum to be at his best on the offensive end.

In the next 27 games he played following his return from COVID-19, he averaged 24.1 points, 6.7 rebounds, and 4.5 assists. Of course, he needed to score and pass more because the Celtics were still recovering from the injury that Kemba Walker suffered that season. However, the most surprising part about Tatum's post-COVID games was that, other than how he was not defending as well as he did a year ago, his shooting numbers dropped because he not only shouldered the offense more but also because he was still physically trying to get back into shape.

However, Jayson Tatum steadily got his rhythm back as the season progressed, and the Celtics needed him to produce more to make a run at a good playoff seed. One of the games that showed that he was probably already back to his old self was when he scored a new career-high of 53 points while also grabbing ten rebounds in a win over the Minnesota Timberwolves on April 9. Since that game, it became customary for Tatum to explode for high-scoring nights

Shortly after that career game against the Wolves, Tatum showcased his superstar quality when he had 44 points and ten rebounds in a win over Golden State Warriors on April 17. Then, in the next game, he had his first triple-double that season when he went for 14 points, 13 rebounds, and ten assists in a loss to the Chicago Bulls.

On April 30, knowing how important it was for the Celtics to win their next few games to avoid the play-in tournament introduced that season, he led Boston to come back from a 32-point deficit against the San Antonio Spurs while also etching his name in franchise lore. In that win for the Celtics, he exploded for a new career-high of 60 points while making 20 of his 37 shots to tie Larry Bird for the franchise record for most points scored in a single game.

Despite his efforts, Tatum could not keep his team out of the play-in tournament because of their injuries. Fellow All-Star Jaylen Brown had to miss the rest of the season early in May. Because of that, Tatum was the lone healthy star on a team that was certainly not as competitive as in previous years since he arrived in Boston. But Jayson Tatum cemented the Boston Celtics' place in the playoffs when he scored 50 points in the play-in tournament win over the Washington Wizards as they ended the regular season with the seventh seed in the East.

Jayson Tatum's scoring numbers jumped to 26.4 points during that season while retaining much of the same efficiency he had a year ago. The late push he had during the latter part of the season allowed him to make the jump from All-Star to legitimate superstar as he was finally healthy following the effects of COVID-19 on his system. On top of improving his scoring numbers, Tatum also finished with career-highs of 7.4 rebounds and 4.3 assists for the Boston Celtics.

However, in the playoffs, Jayson Tatum was a one-player show against a legitimate title contender with three superstars in Kevin Durant, James Harden, and Kyrie Irving. It was Tatum against the world when the Celtics faced the Brooklyn Nets super team in the first round. And it became apparent in the first two games that Jayson Tatum could not do it all for his depleted team.

After the humiliating losses in Games 1 and 2, especially after scoring only nine points in Game 2, Tatum carried the team on his back in Game 3 to avoid a 0-3 hole that was always insurmountable. He finished with 50 points in that game and became the first Celtics player to score 50 or more points in a playoff game since Isaiah Thomas did it a few years ago. He was also the third-youngest player in NBA history to score 50 or more points in a playoff game. Tatum also became only the sixth Celtics player to score 50 or more points in a playoff game, even though the franchise is rich in some of the greatest players the league has ever seen.

As great as Jayson Tatum was in that Game 3 win, his greatness was overshadowed by the greatness of three other superstars. He may have scored a combined total of 72 points in Games 4 and 5, but the Nets just had too much firepower for Tatum to overcome as the Boston Celtics were booted out of the first round in just five games after making it to the conference finals a year ago. This was also the first time in Tatum's four-year career that he could not make it past the first round of the playoffs.

Despite the early exit from the playoffs and the apparent problems that the Boston Celtics had with the chemistry and health of their roster, it was evident that Jayson Tatum was now a superstar who could carry a team on his back. He scored 50 or more points at any given moment whenever he was called to do so. At only 23 years old, he still has plenty of room to grow as the Celtics are looking to rely more on him in the following seasons if they want to get back to championship contention following a disappointing 2020-21 campaign for Boston.

Chapter 5: Personal Life

Jayson Tatum was born and raised in St. Louis, Missouri, to parents born and raised in that area. His mother, Brandy Cole, is a lawyer. She raised him almost on her own after having him when she was just 19. Cole finished her undergraduate studies and got her law degree while taking care of Jayson Tatum when he was still young.

Meanwhile, Jayson's father is Justin Tatum, who himself was also a professional basketball player. Justin Tatum was a muscular and athletic 6'7" power forward who played for Saint Louis in college. He helped his team win a conference title during his three-year college career. He went on to play overseas when Jayson was still a young boy. And after returning, he became an athletics director at Soldan International Studies High School before becoming a basketball coach at Christian Brothers College High School in St. Louis.

Jayson Tatum's godfather is Larry Hughes, a very close friend and former college teammate of his father back in high school and college at Saint Louis University. Hughes was the reason why Tatum could meet LeBron James back in 2006 when the young man from St. Louis was still eight years old. Jayson Tatum is also a cousin of former NBA player and former Cleveland Cavaliers head coach Tyronn Lue.

Another NBA personality with whom Jayson Tatum and his family are close is Bradley Beal, who grew up just a few blocks away from Tatum and his mother. While the Beal family itself was a big household, they were much more into football than basketball. As such, Bradley Beal grew up treating Jayson Tatum as his little brother in basketball. Even after they became NBA players, they still keep in touch from time to time.

Jayson Tatum is in a relationship with Toriah Lachell, with whom he has a baby boy. Tatum's son is named Jayson Christopher Tatum Jr., but the father often calls the little boy "Deuce," another way of calling a two-point basket in basketball.

Growing up, Jayson Tatum idolized Kobe Bryant so much that he wanted to be like him. He patterned his game after Kobe and tried his best to emulate moves we only see Bryant doing. Tatum also used Kobe Bryant's signature shoes. And during summer 2018, he finally got a chance to train together with his childhood hero. Tatum's love for Bryant affected him a lot when the Laker great passed away late in January of 2020.

Jayson Tatum is also fond of watching other star wings such as Carmelo Anthony and Paul George (who himself grew up idolizing Kobe). That is why you see many different star wings in the way Tatum plays the game, as he does not merely rely on emulating Bryant's style but also some of the greats that the league has seen since Kobe's prime.

Chapter 6: Impact on Basketball

It is not uncommon for anyone to ask whether or not a young player such as Jayson Tatum, who is in his early years in the NBA, has already had a significant impact on basketball. Other than the fact that he is one of the younger players in the NBA, he has yet to hit his strides regarding his basketball skills and ability to play at an All-Star level.

Nevertheless, Jayson Tatum has impacted basketball, especially since he fits the bill as the ideal wing player that any team should have in today's NBA brand of basketball, which continues to evolve and change at a rapid pace. His style of play and physical attributes allow him to become the type of player that fits the prototype wing player a contending and versatile team should have in this modern era.

Standing more than 6'8' and with long arms almost seven feet in length, Jayson Tatum has the attributes of a player who could play either forward position. On top of that, he is athletic, mobile, and graceful when running up and down the court. The way he moves like a guard on both offense and defense makes him the ideal type of player in today's position-less and pace-and-space era of NBA basketball.

Because of his height and length, teams can play him at either of the forward positions without losing a bit of productivity. On offense, he has enough versatility in him to play inside and outside. He can create shots off the dribble and can shoot over smaller perimeter defenders guarding him. And when he is playing power forward in a small-ball lineup, he can blow by his bigger but slower defenders or take them out of the paint to stretch the floor so that his teammates can have more driving lanes.

As Jayson Tatum continues to develop into a small forward with the guard skills and shot creation abilities of Kobe Bryant, he has become a virtual matchup nightmare that has proven to be too difficult for opposing teams to contain. One case was when he had 60 during the 2020-21 regular season and when he poured in 50 in the 2021 playoffs. And if he continues to learn how to become a better passer, he can even move down to the shooting guard position to create more mismatches for smaller guards who cannot contest his shot.

It is on the defensive end of the floor where Jayson Tatum becomes even more of a prototypical wing that matches the demands of today's era of position-less basketball. Because teams are now putting more emphasis on ball movement, floor spacing, and three-point shooting, there is a lot of switching happening on the defensive end of the floor. You now often see bigger players switching out on perimeter ball-handlers to try to cover them off the pick-and-roll as quickly as possible.

While such a defensive strategy helps take away the ball-handler's ability to instantly break the defense down off the pick-and-roll either by going straight to the basket or finding daylight to shoot the ball, it creates mismatches. Bigger guys are out on the perimeter trying to contain the likes of Stephen Curry or Kyrie Irving after a pick switched them out of the paint and onto the ball-handler. And in the same instances, you will see guards trying to defend bigger players in the paint because of the switching.

That said, switching on the defensive end might help defend the pick-and-roll, but it is still a very risky strategy because it creates a lot of mismatches on the floor. It is going to be very dangerous if the opposing team can find such mismatches and exploit them. Guards will take big men off the dribble while big men can use their size to score inside against guards.

However, a player like Jayson Tatum allows teams to switch out on defense while minimizing the dangers of creating defensive mismatches. That is because Tatum is a defensive player that can cover both big men and guards. He has the height and length that allow him to defend power forwards well enough inside the paint. Meanwhile, he has the mobility, lateral movement, and length to contain guards out on the perimeter.

If a team wants to be effective when switching on the defensive end, a player like Jayson Tatum is the perfect wing to have because he can defend positions 1 to 4 on the court when he is switching. That is why the Boston Celtics have been very successful on the defensive end since they drafted Jayson Tatum in 2017.

Suppose you look at the Celtics' roster. They have several athletic and mobile players 6'7" or taller because they are much like Jayson Tatum in the sense that they are as close as possible to the prototypical wing needed in the NBA today. Jayson Tatum and Jaylen Brown are both switchable on the defensive end because they can hold their own against guards and big men alike. That is why Tatum has become such an essential defensive asset for the Celtics.

And on offense, players like Jayson Tatum are just as versatile because they can practically play in and out of the perimeter. They stretch the floor, move well without the ball, and make plays for open teammates as well. As such, versatility has become the name of the game in today's NBA. In that regard, it is a game that Jayson Tatum plays well and is still quickly improving on that end of the floor.

It certainly will not be surprising if, several years from now, we equate the definition of what it is to become switchable both on offense and defense to Jayson Tatum. He and several other players have impacted the game in such a way that it has made them the prototype wings any team should be lucky and happy enough to have.

In short, by playing a style that you usually see guards playing and having the physical qualities of a player that can play both forward positions, Jayson Tatum has made an impact on the way we know the importance of prototypical wings that are versatile and switchable on both ends of the floor. Many teams are now trying to find their version of a Jayson Tatum, not just on defense but also offense.

That said, Jayson Tatum is proof that it certainly is effective for teams to have capable and versatile wings that can virtually play any position out there on the floor. Tatum has impacted Celtics basketball by becoming the type of player they could count on to provide a lot of versatility on both ends of the floor. He might even be the only player on the roster capable of doing that at a high level because Kyrie Irving is not someone you could count on to defend bigger players. Gordon Hayward is not the type of star that could shut down point guards out on the perimeter.

In a sense, Jayson Tatum's impact as a basketball player has allowed the Boston Celtics to secure their future. He is someone who almost perfectly fits what it means to play the wing position in this modern NBA era of position-less basketball we are in right now. Another impact he has had on basketball can be seen in how he has given the Celtics, arguably the NBA's most storied franchise, a security blanket for their future. There is no doubt that he is Boston's brightest young star heading into the next ten years or so.

After the Kyrie Irving era in the Boston Celtics history did not pan out well for the franchise, they could rebuild and still contend with Tatum as the focal point of their efforts heading into the future. So long as he stays healthy and happy in Boston, he will undoubtedly remain the face of the franchise. And as Jayson Tatum continues to develop and evolve with the Boston Celtics and a consistently changing NBA style of play, we will eventually see him making a bigger impact on basketball and the way the sport is being played.

Chapter 7: Legacy and Future

Has Jayson Tatum played and done enough in the NBA at this early stage in his career to have already carved a legacy? Perhaps not. But the optimistic part about all of this is that Jayson Tatum has shown enough talent and potential to become one of those rare players that could create a lasting legacy in the NBA. But as of now, he is just a player trying to impact the NBA while stepping into the shoes of former legends and continuing legacies that have started decades ago.

If you look at Jayson Tatum's game, there are many similarities between him and the late great Kobe Bryant. Both are tall and long athletes that like to shoot midrange jumpers over the top of defenses. Using crafty dribble moves or supreme footwork, both players know how to create enough separation out on the perimeter to rise for a shot off the dribble. They also are fierce competitors that love to play big-time moments while hitting big-time shots.

In that sense, Jayson Tatum is one of the few guys in the league who follows the legacy of pure-scoring versatile wings that Kobe Bryant carried for two decades. Bryant himself inherited such a legacy from legends Michael Jordan, Clyde Drexler, and Julius Erving.

As such, Tatum is the type of player that can carry such a legacy into the future. He has patterned his game after Kobe the same way that Bryant patterned his game after Michael Jordan and can take things to the next level. He is bigger and longer than any of his predecessors and is playing in an era with more freedom and spacing for him to operate and score.

He might very well be the next coming of Kobe Bryant or the next iteration of what a high-scoring wing player should look like in today's modern style of NBA basketball. However, Jayson Tatum is still as pure of a scorer and as talented of a young star as his predecessors were when they had just entered the league. His potential to be as great as them and continue one of the greatest legacies in basketball is as high as any other.

The gold standards for scoring wings in today's NBA game are still Kawhi Leonard, Kevin Durant, and Paul George, who also idolized Kobe Bryant growing up. But there is no doubt that Jayson Tatum is on his way to take the torch from those star wing players and to take it farther into the future. And if everything goes right for him, he might even turn out to be just as good as or even better than the man he grew up idolizing.

Concerning that, Jayson Tatum is also one of the flag bearers of the NBA's youth movement. With the likes of young stars such as Ben Simmons, Donovan Mitchell, and Luka Doncic, Tatum continues a legacy of young and talented stars that have been touted as "the future of the NBA" early in their careers.

We saw guys like LeBron James and Kevin Durant earning the media's attention as the next big names in NBA basketball more than a decade ago. And if you look at their careers now, they certainly deserved to be the flag bearers of their youth movement back when they were still up-and-coming young stars in the NBA. To some extent, and even though injuries derailed his career, we also saw Derrick Rose getting called the future of the NBA when he won the MVP in only his third season in the league. Then, after changing the game, Stephen Curry joined LeBron James as the two most influential players in their era. And, of course, who can ever argue that Giannis Antetokounmpo is quickly living up to his name as the next big thing in the NBA?

That said, Jayson Tatum is one of the few young stars in the NBA right now who carry such a legacy of upstart young stars. At this early stage in his career, he is still making a name for himself as one of the best young superstars in the league, but he certainly is on his way to the pedestal as one of the greatest players of today's era. He is young and talented and has a lot of potential to be great. This was shown when he was named an All-Star for the first time in 2020.

And if he can keep improving at a rapid pace, we might even see him becoming one of the faces of the NBA heading into the future. Former young stars such as James, Durant, Rose, and Antetokounmpo made themselves the headliners of their respective youth eras.

Finally, Jayson Tatum is undoubtedly the flag carrier of one of the greatest legacies in professional sports. He is the brightest young star on the Boston Celtics, the team regarded as arguably the most storied franchise in basketball. The Celtics have always been one of the more recognized names in the NBA's history, and there are good reasons for that.

This brand of excellence in Boston Celtics basketball started with Bill Russell back in the late '50s and '60s when he won more than a decade's worth of NBA championships for his team and the likes of legends such as Bob Cousy, Tom Heinsohn, Sam Jones, and John Havlicek. The brand of excellence that he started continued on every decade.

In the '70s, we saw Celtics great John Havlicek, Dave Cowens, and Jo Jo White carrying the torch that Bill Russell lit back in the '60s. Those players also won titles for the Boston Celtics in that era. Then, after that, they passed the torch down to Larry Bird, who won championships together with Celtics legends Kevin McHale and Robert Parish and brought NBA basketball to an entirely new level during the '80s, mainly because of the rivalry between his team and the Los Angeles Lakers. While many still say that Bill Russell is the greatest Celtic in history because of the championships he won and legacies he started, some would say that Bird is the greatest individual Celtics player concerning talent and personal accomplishments.

Though the Boston Celtics saw lean years during the '90s when they did not have a designated star to carry the team during that era, the team saw a resurgence during the 2000s thanks to the rise of pure scorer Paul Pierce. And in the final years of that decade, we saw Pierce competing for championships together with Kevin Garnett, Ray Allen, and Rajon Rondo. In 2008, that squad won the most recent Boston Celtics championship banner.

Tatum is carrying one of the greatest franchise legacies in the game. The stars that led the Boston Celtics in the past were some of the greatest players the league has ever seen. And they were not only great individual players because they won championships for the franchise when they were leading the Boston Celtics.

Though such a burden is too large for any ordinary player, Jayson Tatum is anything but ordinary. Time and time again, he has shown the world that he is one of the most talented young players in the NBA today.

That is more than enough for him to prove that he has enough potential to be the future face of the Boston Celtics franchise when he eventually inherited from the All-Star players the team had before he arrived.

Though it is too early to say that Jayson Tatum can be regarded as one of the best players in the franchise's history, it is safe to say that he has the mindset, talent, and potential to reach heights that his Celtics predecessors were able to achieve. And what that means for Tatum is that he might not only become an NBA star in the future but could also very well be an NBA champion somewhere down the road.

Final Word/About the Author

I was born and raised in Norwalk, Connecticut. Growing up, I could often be found spending many nights watching basketball, soccer, and football matches with my father in the family living room. I love sports and everything that sports can embody. I believe that sports are one of the most genuine forms of competition, heart, and determination. I write my works to learn more about influential athletes in the hopes that from my writing, you the reader can walk away inspired to put in an equal if not greater amount of hard work and perseverance to pursue your goals. If you enjoyed *Jayson Tatum: The Inspiring Story of One of Basketball's Rising Stars,* please leave a review! Also, you can read more of my works on *David Ortiz, Mike Trout, Bryce Harper, Jackie Robinson, Aaron Judge, Odell Beckham Jr., Bill Belichick, Serena Williams, Rafael Nadal, Roger Federer, Novak Djokovic, Richard Sherman, Andrew Luck, Rob Gronkowski, Brett Favre, Calvin Johnson, Drew*

Brees, J.J. Watt, Colin Kaepernick, Aaron Rodgers, Peyton Manning, Tom Brady, Russell Wilson, Odell Beckham Jr., Bill Belichick, Charles Barkley, Trae Young, Gregg Popovich, Pat Riley, John Wooden, Steve Kerr, Brad Stevens, Red Auerbach, Doc Rivers, Erik Spoelstra, Michael Jordan, LeBron James, Kyrie Irving, Klay Thompson, Stephen Curry, Kevin Durant, Russell Westbrook, Anthony Davis, Chris Paul, Blake Griffin, Kobe Bryant, Joakim Noah, Scottie Pippen, Carmelo Anthony, Kevin Love, Grant Hill, Tracy McGrady, Vince Carter, Patrick Ewing, Karl Malone, Tony Parker, Allen Iverson, Hakeem Olajuwon, Reggie Miller, Michael Carter-Williams, John Wall, James Harden, Tim Duncan, Steve Nash, Draymond Green, Kawhi Leonard, Dwyane Wade, Ray Allen, Pau Gasol, Dirk Nowitzki, Jimmy Butler, Paul Pierce, Manu Ginobili, Pete Maravich, Larry Bird, Kyle Lowry, Jason Kidd, David Robinson, LaMarcus Aldridge, Derrick Rose, Paul George, Kevin Garnett, Chris Paul, Marc Gasol, Yao Ming, Al Horford, Amar'e

Stoudemire, DeMar DeRozan, Isaiah Thomas, Kemba Walker, Chris Bosh, Andre Drummond, JJ Redick, DeMarcus Cousins, Wilt Chamberlain, Bradley Beal, Rudy Gobert, Aaron Gordon, Kristaps Porzingis, Nikola Vucevic, Andre Iguodala, Devin Booker, John Stockton, Jeremy Lin, Chris Paul, Pascal Siakam, Gordon Hayward, Nikola Jokic, Bill Russell, Victor Oladipo, Luka Doncic, Ben Simmons, Shaquille O'Neal, Joel Embiid, Donovan Mitchell, Damian Lillard and *Giannis Antetokounmpo* in the Kindle Store. If you love basketball, check out my website at claytongeoffreys.com to join my exclusive list where I let you know about my latest books and give you lots of goodies.

Like what you read? Please leave a review!

I write because I love sharing the stories of influential athletes like Jayson Tatum with fantastic readers like you. My readers inspire me to write more so please do not hesitate to let me know what you thought by leaving a review! If you love books on life, basketball, or productivity, check out my website at claytongeoffreys.com to join my exclusive list where I let you know about my latest books. Aside from being the first to hear about my latest releases, you can also download a free copy of *33 Life Lessons: Success Principles, Career Advice & Habits of Successful People*. See you there!

Clayton

References

[i] Forgrave, Reid. "'Built for basketball': Jayson Tatum was born and raised to be an NBA star". *Bleacher Report*. 19 June 2017. Web.

[ii] Squadron, Alex. "Business is business: Jayson Tatum was sent to destroy your favorite team". *SLAM online*. 11 October 2018. Web.

[iii] Snow, Taylor. "Tatum's childhood shooting session with James comes full circle". *NBA.com*. 23 May 2018. Web.

[iv] "It's not hype if you can do it, and Chaminade's Jayson Tatum can." *Fox Sports*. 15 January 2015. Web.

[v] Biancardi, Paul. "Jayson Tatum commits to Duke". *ESPN*. 13 July 2015. Web.

[vi] Gross, Nick. "Celtics' Jayson Tatum shares great story on Coach K calling him out during Duke game". *NBC Sports*. 12 March 2019. Web.

[vii] "Jayson Tatum". *Draft Express*. Web.

[viii] "Jayson Tatum". *NBADraft.net*. Web.

[ix] Yang, Nicole. "Here's what Brad Stevens had to say about Jayson Tatum's Summer League play". *Boston.com*. 12 July 2017. Web.

[x] Forsberg, Chris. "LeBron James tips cap to Jayson Tatum: 'He's built for stardom'". *ESPN*. 28 May 2018. Web.

[xi] Albertie, Quenton. "Jayson Tatum is working out with Kobe Bryant". *USA Today*. 27 July 2018. Web.

[xii] Felt, Hunter. "Jayson Tatum trains with Penny Hardaway and Kobe Bryant". *Forbes*. 18 September 2018. Web.

[xiii] Dubin, Jared. "How Jayson Tatum changed his game and became a star". *ABC News*. 21 February 2020. Web.

[xiv] "Celtics' Jayson Tatum reacts to death of 'hero, idol' Kobe Bryant". *NBC Sports*. 27 January 2020. Web.

[xv] "Boston Celtics' Jayson Tatum on Kobe Bryant's death: 'It's still heavy on our heart, and people are still thinking about it'". *Massachusetts Live*. 30 January 2020. Web.

[xvi] Malloy, Dallas. "Boston Celtics: Jayson Tatum has taken the superstar leap". *Fan Sided*. 25 April 2021. Web.

Made in United States
North Haven, CT
22 December 2022

29997535R00085